You Haven't Taught Until They Have Learned:

John Wooden's Teaching Principles and Practices

"*You Haven't Taught Until They Have Learned* does a great job of intertwining Swen's experiences with the teaching of Coach Wooden on the hardwood, the classroom, and in life. I think the connection between teaching and coaching is right on, as they are both the same. Coach Wooden was a teacher first. I would recommend this book to teachers, coaches, parents, business executives, and anybody that would want to be more organized and understand how to pay more attention to effort and detail."

— Ann Meyers Drysdale, four-time Kodak All-American at UCLA, 1976 Olympian, first female inductee into the Basketball Hall of Fame, and current *ESPN* women's basketball analyst

"This book wows the mind and gives us a new and different perspective on Coach Wooden as a teacher. Good teaching is identified by its results, by what students learn, and achieved by relentless efforts to improve. By these measures, John Wooden was a master. What this book gives us is a useful and interesting case study of Wooden the teacher: the knowledge, skill, judgment, and commitment to improving his own practice that made him what he is. It should be read by anyone who is a teacher, which, as Wooden reminds us, is all of us."

— James Stigler (professor of psychology, UCLA, & CEO of LessonLab) & Jim Hiebert (Rodney Sharp professor of education, University of Delaware), authors of *The Teaching Gap*

"Whether you're an educator, business entrepreneur, serving in a professional field, community leader, or simply possess a desire to be more effective in organization and leadership, *You Haven't Taught Until They Have Learned* has captured the secrets of Coach John Wooden's strategies. The teaching principles and practices can be converted from the classroom and the basketball court to self-improvement and improved effectiveness. Through observing, studying, interviewing, and examining Coach Wooden's methods, co-authors Swen Nater and Ronald Gallimore share how the reader can become more effective and gain peace of mind through self-satisfaction."

— Roger Dickinson, executive director, Indiana Basketball Hall of Fame

You Haven't Taught Until They Have Learned:

John Wooden's Teaching Principles and Practices

Swen Nater
Ronald Gallimore

Fitness Information Technology

A Division of the International Center
for Performance Excellence
262 Coliseum, WVU-PE
PO Box 6116
Morgantown, WV 26506-6116

Library of Congress Card Catalog Number: 2005931394

ISBN: 1-885693-66-4

Production Editor: Matt Brann
Cover Design: Stephen J. Beard
Typesetter: Jamie Merlavage
Developmental Editor: Matt Brann
Proofreader: Corey Madsen
Indexer: Corey Madsen
Printed by: Data Reproductions

Cover photo © UCLA Photography

10 9 8 7 6 5 4 3 2

Fitness Information Technology
A Division of the International Center for Performance Excellence
West Virginia University
262 Coliseum, WVU-PE
PO Box 6116
Morgantown, WV 26506-6116
800.477.4348 (toll free)
304.293.6888 (phone)
304.293.6658 (fax)
Email: icpe@mail.wvu.edu
Website: www.fitinfotech.com

Dedication

To Marlene Nater and Sharon Gallimore

Table of Contents

Foreword

There must be some mistake here. Swen Nater has co-authored a book about his college basketball coach's teaching methods? Is this someone's idea of a bad joke?

I was Swen's teammate during that golden era at UCLA with Coach John Wooden, forming a relationship and friendship with him that began 35 years ago. But if anyone had ever suggested to me at that time that Swen would one day team up with a UCLA professor to co-author a book detailing the techniques and methodology of our legendary college basketball coach and how he got us to learn what he was trying to teach us, the only natural response would be to immediately call the authorities. If that were indeed to happen, then everything that I know to be true and possible would have to be thrown out the window as utterly useless. If one were to go back in time the more than three decades it has been since Swen and I left UCLA, the only thing less likely to happen than Swen co-authoring a book about the value of Coach Wooden's teaching principles and practices would be me becoming a television commentator and public speaker. I guess it shows that we have both come a long way since our days together at UCLA.

Swen had a ways to go as a basketball player when he first arrived at UCLA. Sure he had a terrific body, and what power, but in that era of basketball, quickness, skill, and timing were far more valuable commodities. When I reflect on those glorious times we shared at UCLA, both on and off the court, the things that stand out about Swen were that he spent all of his time either in the weight room—pounding steel to his never-ending mantra, "I'm going to kill Walton today"—or thinking up what only he could ever consider to be catchy one-liners. If you ever saw Swen play basketball early in his UCLA career, and then compared his timing on the court to his delivery of his jokes, your only possible conclusion would be that Jay Leno had a lot more to be concerned with than any real ball player.

But something happened to Swen during those three marvelous years in Westwood from 1970-73—he was exposed to a master teacher and was taught how to learn, think, and analyze. He also learned how to dream, philosophize, and create. During those magical times, Swen was around a selfless, humble, giving, caring, and loving soul every day—one who saw life as a responsibility to make the world a better place for others and that the strength and character of the individuals in that world were the building blocks. That master teacher was John Robert Wooden.

And now Swen, after all these days gone by, has co-authored the first book to focus exclusively on John Wooden's teaching methods. Swen, like everyone who was under Coach Wooden's supervision, has been able to build a successful life beyond the game of basketball. In this fabulous and important book, *You Haven't Taught Until They Have Learned: John Wooden's Teaching Principles and Practices*, Swen and co-author Ronald Gallimore have broken down, chapter by chapter, the complete structure and keys to Coach Wooden's brilliant, effective, and life-changing teaching capabilities.

The book, with meticulous precision and detail, takes readers step-by-step through how Coach Wooden was able to build relationships with his students and players; how he was able to motivate, drive, and inspire; and how he was able to prepare his lessons, practices, and teaching strategies.

But why should anyone pay attention to Swen Nater, someone who in college never really played any meaningful minutes in games? While Coach Wooden certainly supervised his share of superstars, my experience with the John Wooden phenomenon is that the non-descript pupils are the real heroes of this saga. They were the ones who made the greatest sacrifices but whose rewards were the most ephemeral. They were the ones who most often had the longest journey ahead of them.

That is why Swen's story really is one of the greatest stories ever told. It would be difficult to make up a more unlikely story than Swen's rise to glory both on and off the basketball court. And his success is due in large part to the teaching methods of Coach Wooden, which are detailed in *You Haven't Taught Until They Have Learned.*

Swen did not grow up with a silver spoon in his mouth. Born in Holland, he and his older sister, Rene, were sent to a local orphanage when he was only 6 years old after his financially strapped family moved to America and was only able to take Swen's younger brother with them. Of the 60 other children at the orphanage, Swen and his sister were the only ones there whose parents were still living.

After Swen's parents settled in Southern California, some of their new friends learned of the plight of their two children left behind in Holland and decided to do something about it. As can only happen in Hollywood, Swen and his sister were reunited with their parents on the set of the game show, "This Is Your Life." Swen's parents were lured to the show under false pretenses as members of the audience. When they were unexpectedly called up on stage, imagine their surprise when their two young children came walking out of a makeshift windmill, specially constructed for the reunion.

When Swen arrived in the United States at age 9, he didn't speak a word of English. He had also never seen, much less heard of, the game of basketball. But Swen was soon the tallest lad in school. When he was a junior at Long Beach Wilson High School, he tried out for the basketball team but was cut and told not to come back.

When he graduated from high school, he enrolled at Cypress Community College to pursue a career in mathematics. While walking to math class one day, Swen—now a strapping 6-foot-10—was spotted by the assistant basketball coach, Tom Lubin. Swen was quickly hustled into the office of Cypress head coach Don Johnson, who just happened to have been an All-America basketball player under Coach Wooden at UCLA in the 1950s.

Initially, Swen played very little at Cypress. But through relentless effort, a driving work ethic, and wonderful mentoring from Johnson, by Swen's second year at Cypress he was a Junior College All-American. One fateful day, the Cypress Chargers played the UCLA freshman team at Pauley Pavilion in the lead-in to the UCLA varsity game. Coach Wooden sat by himself in the stands that night and watched Swen dominate the game. They met afterwards for the first time and, after subsequent talks, Coach Wooden agreed to give Swen a scholarship to UCLA, but made it very clear to Swen that he would probably never play in games. That mattered little to Swen, who only wanted a chance to be a part of something special—a member of a team and family, something he was deprived of as a child.

Coach Wooden's proclamation that Swen would only have a limited opportunity to play at UCLA was prophetic. But despite rarely playing in games for the Bruins (who never lost a game while he was a member of that team), Swen, like all of Coach Wooden's students, was beginning to develop both on and off the court. When Swen became the first member of his family to graduate from college, it was only the beginning of his success.

Amazingly, after his days at UCLA concluded, Swen went on to a 12-year professional career that spanned three leagues—the ABA, NBA, and Italian League, leading all three leagues in rebounding. He was the ABA Rookie of the Year in 1974 and still holds the NBA record for most defensive rebounds in a half with 18.

At the conclusion of his playing career, Swen became a teacher. He started the athletic department at Christian Heritage College, in suburban San Diego. He was the school's athletic director, basketball coach, and algebra teacher. In 1990, he helped lead Christian Heritage to the National Christian College Athletic Association national championship.

Inspired by Coach Wooden and all that he has learned from him, Swen has become so much more than just a basketball coach, mathematician, and former player. He is a published author, a film and video producer, a singer/songwriter/guitar player and a poet—having penned more than 125 poems mostly to, for, and about Coach Wooden, some of which are featured in this book. Today, Swen is an assistant sporting good buyer for Costco Wholesale, a $50-billion enterprise that is the largest corporation of its kind in the world.

Swen has traveled the golden road of unlimited devotion all the way to the end. And in *You Haven't Taught Until They Have Learned*, Swen and Ronald Gallimore have captured perfectly and completely why Coach Wooden's teaching principles and practices have been so successful to so many people in so many walks of life.

By now, Swen has not only assimilated all of Coach Wooden' vast reservoir of knowledge but he has also acquired all the human values and personal characteristics that truly make Coach Wooden so incredible. Like Coach, Swen is a true believer in the maxim that everyone is a teacher to someone. And that is why *You Haven't Taught Until They Have Learned* includes an important message for every reader. While teaching takes many forms, the most important is the example the teacher sets. As Coach Wooden is so apt to tell us, "It's what the teachers are themselves."

I try my best to call Coach Wooden on the phone nearly every day to check in with him and try to gain some more of his wisdom. This master teacher, in his mid-90s, is still outworking everyone decades younger than him. When I do actually catch up with him, he invariably has to wrap things up very quickly. He's always rushing off and cutting me short. As he points out, "I've got to go. Swen's on the other line."

I guess the good news is that since Swen has adopted Coach Wooden's teaching principles and practices, which are detailed in *You Haven't Taught Until They Have Learned*, and implemented them so successfully in his own life, there's still some hope for me!

Bill Walton
UCLA (1974)
Naismith Memorial Basketball Hall of Fame (1993)

Guest Foreword

As a young man living in the Los Angeles area, it seemed impossible to not get caught up in the UCLA phenomenon, it's basketball teams, and, of course, "The Wizard," Coach John Wooden. I watched UCLA win year after year, sometimes with incredible and unequaled talent, and more often with a team that had no apparent superstar. No matter the year, no matter the player caliber, UCLA fans became accustomed to winning a championship, and the Bruins delivered year after year.

I first met John Wooden in 1989 when he attended the NCAA Final Four in Seattle. This was the first tournament he had been to in four years since the death of his beloved wife, Nell. After the championship game, I attended a special dinner with approximately 50 other visiting CEOs of companies around the country. There were enough egos in that room to fill the great outdoors—but when Coach Wooden entered the room you could feel the difference and respect. We all shut up and listened as he spoke to us for 20 minutes.

After the dinner I had the opportunity to speak with Coach Wooden privately and I explained that I was a UCLA fan. "Coach, everyone in this room claims to be a fan," I said, "but I'm the only person here, besides you, who can name the starting five on your first championship team."

Several years later we asked Coach Wooden to attend our annual Costco managers meeting in Seattle to address our group on his philosophy about teaching and winning. I was shocked when, at the conclusion of his remarks, he presented me with a basketball signed by him and the five starters from that first championship team (Walt Hazzard, Fred Slaughter, Keith Erickson, Jack Hirsch, and Gail Goodrich). Talk about a lesson in thoughtfulness and humility—here was that great man bestowing an incredible gift to me.

Many of us are continually struck by the notion that Coach Wooden always thought of himself first and foremost as a teacher. In his mind, more important than the wins, the championship banners, and the acclaim was how effective he had been in teaching his young people how to succeed in life.

As the CEO of a large organization, I—along with my colleagues—am committed to success through fellow employees. Our attitude is that teaching is paramount and that if any manager doesn't understand that teaching is 90% of their job, then they just don't get it!

In *You Haven't Taught Until They Have Learned,* co-authors Swen Nater and Ronald Gallimore do an excellent job of detailing the teaching methods that helped make John Wooden arguably the greatest coach and teacher of our time. Teacher respect, motivation, self-improvement, deep subject knowledge, preparation, and transferring information are qualities all teachers should possess at any level and in any environment. They work on the court as well as in an institution or company.

As an admirer of Coach Wooden since the early 1960s, I am pleased that there is now a roadmap of his teaching principles that can guide us as we continue our travels down the path of success. I never tire of reading about him.

Jim Sinegal
CEO, Costco Wholesale

Preface
A Master Teacher

"When I became a high school teacher, I took my responsibility very seriously. I believed then, and I do now, that I was paid to teach, and that meant it was my responsibility to help every one of my students learn. I believe it's impossible to claim you have taught, when there are students who have not learned. With that commitment, from my first year as an English teacher until my last as UCLA basketball teacher/coach, I was determined to make the effort to become the best teacher I could possibly be, not for my sake, but for all those who were placed under my supervision."[1]

John Wooden is widely regarded as one of the greatest college basketball coaches of all time. In fact, both ESPN and *Sports Illustrated* named him the greatest coach of the 20th Century. The reasons are well known to basketball fans. His UCLA teams won a record 10 NCAA championships (including an incredible seven in a row from 1967-73), 38 straight NCAA tournament victories, 19 conference championships, had an 88-game winning streak over four seasons, and enjoyed four undefeated seasons. He won with teams of great talent and some with relatively less. When he retired from coaching in 1975, he had accumulated an overall record in collegiate coaching of 667 wins and 161 losses, good for an 81 percent winning percentage.

The list of honors bestowed upon Coach Wooden beyond athletics is another testament to his lifetime of accomplishments. Among them include being named the 1974 California "Grandfather of the Year" by the National Father's Day Committee, receiving the 1995 Frank G. Wells Disney award for contributions to teaching, being honored with the 2004 Walk of Hearts Teacher Recognition Award, and, in 2003, receiving the Medal of Freedom, which is awarded by the President and is the highest honor the government can bestow on a citizen of the United States.

While team championships and individual honors are gratifying, it is the teaching and practices that Coach Wooden valued most. In countless speeches he has given before and since his retirement, he surprises audiences when the Basketball Hall of Fame coach prefaces many of his remarks by saying, *"When I was teaching at UCLA ... "*

"I always considered myself a teacher rather than just a coach. Everyone, everyone is a teacher. Everyone is a teacher to someone; maybe it's your chil-

dren, maybe it's a neighbor, maybe it's someone under your supervision in some other way, and in one way or another, you're teaching them by your actions."[2]

Coach Wooden began his career teaching high school English and coaching several sports, doing so for more than 10 years after his graduation from Purdue University, where he was a three-time All-American from 1930-32. He credits much of his success and what he learned about teaching from four influential men in his life—Joshua Hugh Wooden, his father; Earl "Pop" Warriner, his principal and coach at Centerton (Indiana) Elementary School; Glenn Curtis, his coach at Martinsville (Indiana) High School; and Ward "Piggy" Lambert, his coach at Purdue University. He also acknowledges the blessings of his talented students, who helped him learn in his classrooms and on the practice courts.

Coach Wooden believes the fundamental principles of teaching are the same both in the classroom and on the practice court. Teaching academics or athletics, he concludes, is more effective if these fundamental principles are followed. Can teachers, parents, and leaders learn from this master of basketball teaching? We believe the answer is an emphatic, "Yes."

This is a powerful belief, one which brings us to the premise of this book. Not only was Coach Wooden a great coach, he was a master teacher. In fact, he was a great coach because he was a master teacher. What he has learned from others in the classroom and perfected on the practice court are fundamental principles and practices of effective teaching. These have a timeless and universal quality, applicable to all teaching situations—the classroom, the home, the workplace, and everywhere that a person has the responsibility for helping others learn and excel. Coach Wooden's approach—his principles and practices—can be studied and applied by teachers, coaches, parents, and anyone else who is responsible for, works with, or supervises others.

Some may think this is a bold claim, but it is a claim that rests on Coach Wooden's teaching accomplishments. So what does the record say about him as a teacher?

First of all, there are the impressive achievements of his students—the UCLA players he taught to play so well that for more than a decade they dominated their sport as no other collegiate teams have ever done. Many of these individuals went on to distinguished professional basketball careers.

But it is not the success of these superstar players that best reveals the effectiveness of Coach Wooden's teaching. His commitment to teaching was not limited to those who did the scoring. His commitment was to help all students under his supervision, even those who seldom played in games and on whose practice efforts his teaching depended, reach their individual potential.

He needed the reserves for his teaching to work. His system of basketball allowed only seven or eight players, out of twelve, to participate in meaningful game action (before the outcome was clearly decided). Yet, it also required that reserve players be highly motivated and eager to learn so that they challenged the starters every day in practice. Without the edge of competitive practices that the reserves provided, Coach Wooden knew he could not push the starters to achieve the excellence that led to 10 NCAA championships. It might be expected that the motivation and attention of these reserve players would wane since they knew they had little chance of earning significant playing time. Yet many responded to his teachings and worked hard in practice to learn, improve, and push the starters as hard as they could.

Evidence of Coach Wooden's impact as a teacher is also reflected in the success of his former players away from basketball. Many of his former players have gone on to become successful physicians, attorneys, business executives, coaches, and teachers. The list of accomplished professionals is long and impressive, and perhaps composes the best evidence a teacher such as him could have in proving that his teaching made a difference. The success of his players beyond basketball is a great source of satisfaction for him.

One of his favorite poems ("They Ask Me Why I Teach," by Glennice L. Harmon), begins with these lines:

They ask me why I teach
And I reply,
Where could I find more splendid company?
"When I think of all the attorneys that played for me and the doctors that played for me ... the dentists that played for me ... the teachers that played for me ... the businessmen that played for me ... it's good. Their joys are my joys.
Their sorrows and disappointments were my sorrows and disappointments.
I'm happy that not a day goes by without a call from one of my players."[3]

Dozens of Coach Wooden's former players will testify that the lessons he taught extend far beyond the basketball court. Yes, they learned to play well, but they also learned to live well through the values he taught and, more importantly, lived up to. He was their teacher in the truest sense of the word.

But his players were not his only students. He has become a teacher to a much larger audience. When Coach Wooden turned 93 on October 14, 2003, Bill Dwyre, a sports columnist for the *Los Angeles Times*, captured the kind of teacher he had become to the nation.

"To not celebrate, to fail to take notice, would be unthinkable. It has been 28 years since he stopped coaching UCLA's basketball team, 28 years since the last of those magical 10 national championships. And it has been 28 years of his growing on us, the sports community of Southern California. Of his teaching us perspective, showing us how character counts, patting us on the hand

to assure us that, whatever it is we are all hyped up about, the sun will come up tomorrow. For 28 years, long since the basketball buzz has gone away, he has remained our elder statesman about life."

While Dwyre and others who have had close and extended contact with Coach Wooden have soaked up his teaching principles and practices, those who come in contact with him for just a brief moment also often take away a lifetime of valuable lessons. After a brief trip from Indiana to Los Angeles to meet him, Roger Dickinson, the executive director of the Indiana Basketball Hall of Fame, wrote:

"As I drove to the airport I thought to myself, I had just met the most remarkable person ever in my life. Here is an individual that is a legend in his own time, yet he is humble, wholesome, moral, respected, decent, and honorable and the type of person that anyone would be happy to call Coach, dad, grandpa, friend, counselor or servant of God. Coach Wooden continues to set a standard of excellence that is beyond most people's grasp. He demonstrates every day that by staying active and pushing one's self mentally that life can be good at any age."[4]

While Coach Wooden continues to be a great teacher, he is correct in believing that everyone is a teacher to someone. Anyone who is around people teaches through example or curriculum. Although Coach Wooden taught, and continues to teach well beyond the court or classroom, it is the purpose of this book to focus on his pedagogy, drawing attention to specific principles for effective teaching that can be transferred from the court to anywhere teaching takes place.

Design of the Book

The idea for this book began when Swen called Ronald in the fall of 2002 with an invitation: "Let's write a book about Coach Wooden's teaching." Shortly thereafter, we became a writing team. The goal was to combine the experiences of a former player under Coach Wooden (Swen) with the work of a researcher who had studied Coach Wooden's philosophy and practice (Ronald).

As a three-year student of Coach Wooden (1970-1973), Swen experienced first-hand the teaching principles and practices that are the focus of this book. Because of that and to bring life to the text, we decided early in the writing process to use the first-person voice of Swen throughout the book. To help readers keep track of "who is speaking" throughout the text, from this point on the first-person pronoun always refers to Swen. Coach Wooden's words appear in italics. To illustrate this usage, consider this key question, which it is hoped that the book answers:

How did Coach Wooden keep seldom-used reserves engaged in learning on the practice floor so that they provided the stiff competition for the starters on which his system and success depended? Since I was one of those reserves (backing up three-time NCAA Player of the Year Bill Walton) who rarely played but on whom Coach Wooden depended so much, my story helps answer this question.

During his recruitment of me, Coach Wooden was direct and candid. Here's how he describes what happened:

"'Swen, if you come to UCLA you will play very little in actual games, maybe not at all because I've got someone coming in who is extremely talented [Walton]. However, if you work with us, practice with and against this player, by the time you graduate I feel certain you'll get a pro contract. You'll be that good because of the role you'll play on our team.' Swen listened and joined us."

My story raises an important question. How did Coach persuade me—an impetuous youth—to stick with "the plan" for three years? Somehow he was able to engage and motivate me and focus on what I could learn rather than the immediate rewards most athletes seek. That is an impressive example of successful teaching by any standards.

Skeptics might dismiss the claims of great teaching if the only evidence of success was in the achievements of superstar players—those who are in the Basketball Hall of Fame like Walton and Kareem Abdul-Jabbar (known as Lewis Alcindor when he played for UCLA). It is not so easy to dismiss Coach Wooden's success with someone like me who seldom played in college, yet in the professional game was acknowledged for a mastery of the fundamentals learned at UCLA while "never playing."

Years later, when I became a basketball coach and teacher myself, I began to test Coach Wooden's teaching principles and practices. Whether the subject was basketball, English, or mathematics, I discovered that the universality of Coach's approach proved successful with many different populations. I began to call him for advice and ideas, and over the years discovered that my former coach's teaching principles and practices were woven together into a comprehensive system of education in the classroom, on the court, and in the corporate world. During a long and successful coaching career, through experimentation, careful study, and reflection, Coach Wooden crafted a teaching approach that can help anyone—teachers, coaches, parents, leaders, and anyone in a position of supervision.

Similar conclusions were drawn by Ronald, who researched Coach Wooden's teaching practices for more than 30 years. Throughout the 1974-75 season, Ronald (and his colleague Roland Tharp) sat at center court in UCLA's Pauley Pavilion during practices to systematically record Coach Wooden's acts of teaching.[6] After thousands of observations they concluded that his teaching practices illustrated what research showed to be effective teaching (i.e., well planned, brisk lessons that are information-rich and engaging).

Over the past few years, Ronald has interviewed Coach Wooden on numerous occasions as part of an investigation of the parallels between his teaching practices and contemporary teaching research.[7] He arranged for Wooden to watch and comment on a videotape of a high school team's practice. This material is used in the book to describe Coach Wooden's principles and practices, and to investigate how they do and do not fit with contemporary teaching theory and research.

We are eager to pass along what Coach Wooden taught us both about teamwork and teaching, in one way or another, for a third of a century. The book itself is a team effort of two students who learned from Coach Wooden in two very different ways: one first hand and personal, the other as a detached observer struggling to be objective.

Among the most important of Coach Wooden's principles for success is teamwork. All UCLA basketball players learned that it was the Bruins, not an individual, who scored points in games. No one player was capable of scoring without the passing, screening, and cutting of his teammates. It was a team effort.

"Each of us must make the effort to contribute to the best of our ability according to our individual talents. And then we put all the individual talents together for the highest good of the group. ... Understanding that the good of the group comes first is fundamental to being a highly productive member of a team."[8]

"It's amazing what a team can accomplish when no one cares who receives the credit."[9]

Acknowledgments

Every book has a history. Like any history, a book emerges from many sources and it is difficult to fix a single origin point. This book is no different. The immediate origin was a phone call. Swen was working on the idea for a book about his experiences as a student of Coach John Wooden and how Coach had taught. After drafting some material, he called Coach Wooden for guidance, and he suggested that Swen contact Ron, which he did in September 2003.

After some conversations and exchanges of chapter drafts, we (Swen and Ron) decided that using two very different perspectives on Coach's teaching was a workable concept for a book—one detached and impersonal perspective (Ron as the researcher of Coach Wooden), and one intimate and personal perspective (Swen as the student of Coach Wooden).

Another origin of this book was Roland Tharp's suggestion to Ron in 1974 that they conduct a research study of Coach Wooden's teaching practices. With Wooden's permission, Ron and Roland attended practices during the 1974-75 season, developed a systematic coding scheme, coded more than 3,000 acts of teaching, and drafted an article for publication. Before sending the manuscript to the publisher, Ron and Roland sent it to Coach Wooden for comments. But he never wrote back. The article was published, and except for a few inquiries, it remained for the authors a pleasant memory.[1] In 2001, Ron learned from Marv Alkin (UCLA professor) that Coach Wooden had distributed photocopies of the 1976 article. This was the first time Ron and Roland had any knowledge of Coach's attitude toward the study. Shortly after these events, Tara Scanlan (UCLA professor) suggested that Ron and Roland revisit the original study, update it, and make a presentation at the annual meeting of the Association for the Advancement of Applied Sports Psychology (AAASP). To prepare for the conference, Ron videotaped several interviews with Coach about teaching that updated the original study, and provided information and quotations used in this book.[2]

There were other critical points in this book's history—Coach's invitation to Swen to join the UCLA team, and a phone call in 1948 that came too late. After coaching Indiana State, John Wooden had two job offers, one from the University of Minnesota and the other from UCLA. He wanted to bring assistant coach Eddie Powell with him to his new job; UCLA agreed, but the

Minnesota representative needed to get approval, and promised to call back the next day. Wooden favored the Minnesota job, but promised UCLA he would decide and provide it with an answer by the next day. By the next morning, a blizzard had destroyed the phone lines in Minnesota, preventing the school's representative from being able to call when promised. So when UCLA's representative called that day, Wooden, being true to his word about having an answer, accepted the offer from UCLA. When Minnesota got its phones back in order and the phone call was finally placed, it was too late.[3] John Wooden and Eddie Powell went west and started a legendary chapter in the history of college basketball, and made this book possible.

Some special teachers are also a part of the history of the formation of this book. For Swen, there was Mrs. Rochte, Don Johnson, and Tom Lubin. Like most everyone, Swen remembers Mrs. Rochte as an exceptional journalism and poetry teacher he studied under at Jefferson Middle School in Long Beach, California. Innovative and organized, she taught with only one objective— that all students learn. Don Johnson was Swen's first basketball coach at Cypress College in Cypress, California. An All-American under Coach Wooden, he taught basketball as if he were in a classroom. His explanations and demonstrations were clear and helped Swen, a novice in the sport, grasp the basic concepts of basketball, which ultimately helped him earn an athletic scholarship at UCLA. Tom Lubin, the nephew of Olympic great Frank Lubin, passed on Frank's hook shot and the fundamentals of post play to Swen. Though Swen was very rough around the edges, Tom never gave up. He, along with Mrs. Rochte and Don Johnson, continued to teach until Swen learned.

After completing his years at UCLA and playing 12 years of professional basketball, Swen began to teach college mathematics, physical education, and men's basketball at Christian Heritage College in El Cajon, California. While studying the game and teaching, he realized he had excellent models in his past and began to draw from the experience and knowledge of Don Johnson, Tom Lubin and Coach Wooden.

Two of Ron's special teachers were John Haberland and Lee Sechrest. John picked Ron to be a teaching assistant in an undergraduate class in statistics at the University of Arizona and was the first to suggest graduate school in psychology—and in particular Northwestern University, where John had earned his PhD. At Northwestern University, Lee was Ron's professor and mentor— and still is more than 45 years later. Lee is now, coincidentally, Professor Emeritus at the University of Arizona.

Many individuals helped us blend the two perspectives into a single manuscript. Karen Givvin, Tom Lubin, Jack Keogh, Jim Hiebert, and John Nolan provided helpful comments and suggestions. We especially thank James Stigler, Claude Goldenberg, Ann Meyers Drysdale, and Barbara Keogh for extraordinarily detailed feedback and recommendations. Scott Quintard (UCLA Photography) helped us search the UCLA archives for photographs. UCLA's Center for Culture and Health (http://cultureandhealth.ucla.edu/cch) and LessonLab (http://www.lessonlab.com) supported this effort over the years in many ways, both material and otherwise, and so did many friends and colleagues in both institutions. We are grateful to everyone who helped us and hope the final product is something they feel justified their time and effort.

Our editor at Fitness Information Technology, Matthew Brann, was a major help throughout the process, and we wish to thank him for his patience and many contributions.

Each of us in our own way has been a student of Coach Wooden. The book is one way of thanking him for all that he taught us. We hope he will find it as acceptable as we are grateful for his teachings.

Finally, each of us has a teacher at home from whom we have learned to be better men. Without them, this book would not be possible and it is dedicated to them: Marlene Nater and Sharon Gallimore.

Swen Nater
Ronald Gallimore

Fairness

Every child, in his uniqueness, has a name,
And no other, under Heaven, is the same.
So if teachers would be fair, they should reserve,
The unique and tailored treatment they deserve.

On the surface equal portions may seem fair,
For each child will therefore hold an equal share.
But true "fairness," in the script of higher creeds,
Is when each child holds exactly what he needs.

Swen Nater

Chapter 1

They are all Different:
Teacher-Student Relationships are the Foundation of Effective Teaching

Decades after our UCLA years, many of Coach John Wooden's former players look back in wonderment at how much he taught us. Few doubt we became better players through what he taught, but most believe we became better human beings by *how* he taught. For many, the relationship with Coach Wooden has lasted a lifetime and is a treasure of inestimable value. I am one of many of Coach's former players who believe that my whole life was shaped for the better by the three years I spent as his student.

Those who know Coach only at a distance might assume these relationships were so strong and durable because he was mild-mannered, gentle, kind, and easygoing. But his players know that nothing could be further from the truth. Publicly, he was and is still known as a kind, grandfatherly man. But behind the closed doors of Pauley Pavilion, our home court, he was a strict teacher of the first order.

Ask Coach how he developed enduring teacher-student relationships with high-spirited young men that lasted for a lifetime, and he can tell you exactly how he did it.

"They are all different. There is no formula. I could name players, all who were spirited, but in a different way. You can't work with them exactly the same way. You've got to study and analyze each individual and find out what makes them tick. Some you may have to put on the bench more. Others you've got to pat on the back more. I wish there was a formula. The same thing won't work with every team. It depends on the personnel. The same thing was true

Ever since his early days as the head coach at Indiana State University, Coach Wooden displayed an intense attitude on the practice court, which remained with him during his legendary career at UCLA.

in my English classes. So you have to know the individuals you are working with."[1]

Coach Wooden will quickly add, with understated conviction, that he believes this approach will not only work with today's *athletes*, it will work with *all students*. He believes the principles and practices he used to build teacher-student relationships are tried, true, and timeless. I believe he is right to make this claim based on my experience as a player and student of Coach Wooden.

The process began in the fall of 1970 when I enrolled at UCLA in the middle of a run of national championships unequaled in intercollegiate history. The National Collegiate Athletic Association (NCAA) is the governing body of intercollegiate sports in the United States. Every spring, the NCAA conducts a national basketball tournament of the leading teams from every region of the nation. When I arrived, Coach Wooden's UCLA teams had won titles in 1964, 1965, 1967, 1968, 1969, and 1970. By the time I departed in 1973, the UCLA Bruins had hung three more NCAA championship banners from the rafters of Pauley Pavilion.

But those successes were in the future when I was still in junior college and being recruited by Coach Wooden. On my recruiting visit to UCLA, Coach was candid. Very candid. He told me I would probably never receive much playing time in games, but that I would practice every day against the best college center in the country. He promised the experience would help me reach my potential, provided I put in the effort required.

Although I knew before enrolling at UCLA I would be a backup, that didn't change the reality I faced during my three years on the team. Like all young athletes, I wanted to play in games, but that was not to be. I was backing up Bill Walton, a storied high school player who became a three-time NCAA player of the year. He was dubbed by the media as the leader of the "Walton Gang" that dominated collegiate basketball, winning games by an average of 30 points and putting together two perfect seasons with 30-0 records. For all practical purposes, many of our games were decided before halftime. For the most part, the only playing time I enjoyed was at the end of games when the outcome was no longer in doubt. At times, I became frustrated and discouraged, which put my motivation to practice and learn at risk.

Although I knew what I was getting into by going to UCLA, based on the candid talks I had with Coach during my recruiting visit, that did not diminish the challenge I posed to Coach as he attempted to keep me motivated. Had I elected to walk away, I would not have been the first youthful recruit who found such a commitment too much to bear after the initial excitement of being recruited to UCLA had waned. However, Coach knew he needed to help me understand it was important for the success of the team for me to compete vigorously in practices, all the while knowing I had only the bench to look forward to on game days. Coach knew as talented as Walton was, he would never reach his potential unless I reached mine. And for both of us to progress, Walton and I both needed to be good students on the practice floor and attentive to Coach's instruction.

How Coach Wooden managed to keep me focused on learning and progressing reveals important principles and practices that every teacher can use. These include

- setting challenging expectations matched to each individual's ability and personality,
- getting to know each individual well enough to comprehend what each was capable of achieving,
- truly caring about each as an individual person,
- tailoring instruction and support to individual differences, and
- treating everyone with respect and fairness.

These are hardly new teaching principles or practices. But the way Coach Wooden blended them is worth the attention of any teacher or coach. But that's getting ahead of the story. My introduction to Coach Wooden's approach to building teacher-student relationships began in my first days of practice at UCLA, when I got an early lesson in challenging expectations.

Learning About High Expectations

The first three weeks of practice were devoted to fundamentals and conditioning. After 90 minutes of fundamentals and Xs and Os, we scrimmaged full-court (5-on-5). The UCLA squad consisted of 15 players. Divided into three teams of five—teams A, B, and C—teams A and B were to scrimmage for 20 minutes, while team C shot free throws on side baskets. Teams B and C would then scrimmage for the next 20 minutes, while team A shot free throws. The last 20 minutes, teams A and C scrimmaged, while team B shot free throws. I was on team A.

Besides the application of what we were learning, one purpose of scrimmaging full-court was to accelerate our conditioning and stamina. It was the most physically demanding thing I had ever done. Coach Wooden had only one rule during the scrimmages—unless he blew his whistle to stop action, no player could stop moving or running. There was no resting or standing allowed. Often, this meant several minutes of sprinting and jumping without a rest. About five minutes into the first scrimmage on the first day of practice, I thought someone had sucked all of the air out of Pauley Pavilion. My head began to spin. The pain in my side was so acute I felt like doubling over. I didn't care about Coach's rule anymore. I stopped, hoping the pain would subside. As soon as I stopped, a strong, loud voice (something I imagine a higher power would sound like) emphatically demanded, *"Swen, you are not to stop running! Catch up with the team!"* It was Coach Wooden. The 20-minute session seemed to last an eternity, but thank goodness, it ended and team A's 20 minutes of free throw shooting allowed me to rest while the other two teams competed.

Before I knew it, it was time for my team to start scrimmaging again. I thought to myself, "Does Coach Wooden possess some magical power to speed up time?" There was no way 20 minutes had passed. My side was still hurting and I had barely regained my breath. But the whistle blew and our second scrimmage began. This time it took only 30 seconds for me to feel like I was running a marathon on Mount Everest. The air was gone and replaced by such painful exhaustion I thought I was going to die. Everything was in slow motion. I don't think I scored a point, got one rebound, or made a single pass. It was all I could do to stay on my feet. But no one else had stopped and I wasn't about to be the first to quit. I kept moving, albeit slowly.

Scrimmage was not the only demanding practice segment. Coach Wooden frequently used the infamous "imaginary shooting" drill. Facing the coach, all players assumed a crouching position, ready to shoot an imaginary jump shot with chin up, head directly above the midpoint between the feet, feet a little wider than the shoulders, elbow above the knee and wrinkles in the cocked wrist of the shooting hand. As he blew the whistle, we jumped high into the air and shot an imaginary shot, resumed the initial position, and waited for the whistle to blow again. At first it didn't seem difficult, but after 30 seconds, it felt as though my thighs were going to catch fire. Just before I collapsed, we rested, only to start again 10 seconds later. This routine persisted for about four minutes. All I could think about was, "How am I going to make it through the rest of practice?" My leg strength was so depleted, I could not lift my feet from the ground. When Coach Wooden saw me, he unsympathetically said, *"Swen, jump! Come on! You're not even getting off the ground!"*

Somehow, though, I survived that first practice and then made it through the entire first week. Week two became easier, and by the third week I was in the best physical condition of my life.

But conditioning in Coach Wooden's classroom was not limited to the physical. He also had a plan for helping us successfully handle the mental and emotional challenges a highly competitive game would present, something he called "mental and emotional conditioning." To achieve that, he saw to it that we played and practiced with maximum focus, concentration, and intensity for the entire practice session. For a coach, this is a daunting task, but he pulled it off. For two hours he never let up shouting instructions and immediately correcting every miscue and even the slightest decrease in attention. Even when he stopped practice for short moments of correction, he somehow maintained high learning intensity. *"No, no, no. How many times do I have to tell you? We go guard to guard to shift the defense. Now do it again!"*

We did it again and again, and it still wasn't good enough. *"You didn't cut deep enough to get open. Goodness gracious, how in the world do you expect to get open in the games if you don't do it now? Take him hard to the basket and come out hard. Do it again—this time do it right."*

"Much better," we heard him say, creating a little oasis of relief. But the respite was short-lived. *"But it's not good enough. The ball must swing quicker and the cutter must follow immediately while the defensive guard is off-balance. That way you'll get open. Again, quicker, sharper, better!"*

And he didn't let up. We might repeat that same play 20 times a day and he still wasn't happy. When the allotted time ended for one drill, the next activity was of equal intensity and demand. He wasn't satisfied. It seemed he was on a quixotic quest for perfection and wasn't going to let up until he found it. When we improved in one area of the play, he would pick apart another. Being mentally conditioned to accept nothing less than perfection was frustrating for me because I foresaw no personal success at the end of the tunnel. Why should I continue to work that hard when I was going to be sitting on the bench anyway?

A Life-Long Relationship is Formed

I remember wondering, "What is going on here? Will my entire UCLA career be this miserable? Am I going to have to go through practice after practice with this drill sergeant, feeling like I am not making any progress?"

Then something happened that opened my eyes to what Coach Wooden was trying to do, motivated me to stick with the program, and initiated what grew into a close teacher-student relationship. After several days of pondering his severe instructional methods, I approached him one weekday morning and requested a private conference. My agenda was to receive some sort of encouragement that would provide motivational fuel to keep me going. I needed something that would help me to continue giving maximum effort. What was about to happen gave me much more than I was looking for; it gave me insight into his methods, which eventually led to a dramatic and positive development of our relationship.

Coach invited me to sit and talk in his office and I unloaded my frustration. I expressed how much I wanted to learn, become better at my position, and progress, yet how difficult it was to accomplish those goals while knowing I was destined to sit on the bench. To that point in our relationship, his role in my life was that of a sergeant, but that image quickly changed. His demeanor was more like a father. I felt as though I was in the presence of love and understanding, care and empathy. He listened intently with warm, compassionate eyes fixed on mine, something I didn't expect from a drill sergeant. For that half hour, he made me feel like I was the most important person in the world.

Though I had a new opinion of what my coach was like, when I finished speaking, I still expected him to respond with something to the effect of, "Tough it out and deal with it." After all, it wasn't like I was such a good player that I was indispensable. We had 12 high school and community college All-Americans on the team, all with great talent and impressive résumés. And besides, I realized that I was far behind Walton in my basketball and athletic development. But, to the contrary, Coach Wooden responded with understanding—communicating to me that he knew how I felt. Then he gave me his answer, although it was not the one I was looking for. I was not promised more playing time, but he did give me a valid reason to keep going—he needed me to improve to a level of performance where I would be able to give Walton all he could handle in practice. As good as Walton was, he needed me to challenge him to reach higher levels so he would never face an opposing team's center better than me. Coach asked me if I was ready to handle the challenge and I responded affirmatively. I gave him permission to help me reach our mutual goal. I now had a reason to improve; not the reason I was looking for, but the one I needed at the time. I departed his office encouraged and counting the hours to that afternoon's practice session.

When I walked onto the floor that afternoon one-half hour before the start of practice (as usual), Coach Wooden was already there. I headed to an open basket to begin warming up but looked over at him first. He gave me a smile and nod, and I reciprocated.

I should have anticipated what was about to happen. Once practice began, the understanding, gentle, considerate, caring, sensitive father figure I had spoken with earlier in the day unleashed a two-hour barrage of corrections directed at me, or at least so it seemed. It was worse than before I had met with him! At first I was confused. He had said he wanted me to improve so I could challenge Walton, and now it felt like he was trying to tear me down. I guess I expected him to tone down the corrections a bit; perhaps lower the bar some so I could feel like I was making progress day by day. Instead, it was as if he had raised the standards I was to meet. The motivation I had walked onto the court with that day was fading away fast.

But a small, inner voice reminded me I had given him

Courtesy of Cumberland House Publishing

Nater initially had difficulty remaining motivated while serving as a backup center to Walton, but with the help of Coach Wooden he overcame that hurdle.

permission to do exactly what he was doing. I had given him license to push me as hard as he thought best, so that I in turn could become the most challenging center Bill Walton played against. And so Coach did just that. Errors I made that had gone uncorrected in earlier practices were no longer allowed to pass. Many more mistakes were merely added to the old list of previously corrected errors that I continued to commit. Coach did have some nice things to say now and then. But far more frequent were the quick, succinct instructions as soon as I made an error:

- *"Move your feet; don't reach."*
- *"Keep your hands up when free throws are shot!"*
- *"When you get a rebound, keep the ball high; don't bring it down for a short player to steal!"*
- *"Box out!"*

- *"Turn to the basket as soon as the shot goes up; get ready to rebound!"*
- *"Be quick, but don't hurry."*
- *"Hustle, hustle, hustle!"*
- *"Jump stop like this; not like that; like this [quick demonstration]."*
- *"Goodness gracious sakes Swen, how many times do I have to say it? You are not to dribble the ball!"*

I was not the only recipient of his attentions. Like a rapid-fire gun, he shot corrections at everyone on the team as soon as he saw any error. Of course, these corrections were never allowed to slow down the physically demanding pace of practices. He kept firing corrections and we kept hustling.

A study of Coach Wooden's practices revealed that he made one of these short, pointed corrections about every minute.[2] Although he never lectured or harangued players during practice, he also never stopped correcting, instructing, and demonstrating, all the while demanding that his players perform drills and scrimmages at game speed.

When researchers asked Coach Wooden why he made so many corrections and so seldom praised the players, he answered this way:

"I believe correcting is the positive approach. I believe in the positive approach. Always have."[3]

As a former student who committed many errors during practice and therefore was a recipient of many corrections, it was the "information" embedded in corrections that I needed most. Having received it, I could then make the adjustments and changes needed. It was the information that promoted change. Had the majority of Coach Wooden's corrective strategies been positive ("Good job") or negative ("No, that's not the way"), I would have been left with an evaluation, not a solution. The corrections did not address or attack me as a person. New information was aimed at the act, rather than the actor. In this way, his corrections were positive and far more valuable to me than general statements.

Somehow, as young as I was, I was able to read Coach Wooden's strong criticism as beneficial; I interpreted all the corrections to mean Coach cared enough about me, a reserve, to spend practice time helping me improve. If he had lowered his expectations it would have subtly communicated to me that he didn't think I could improve enough to warrant his time. With Coach now convinced that I was committed to helping the team by challenging Walton, he was free to fulfill his part. I had signaled my acceptance of whatever teaching methods he chose, and from then on he corrected with relish and no restraint.

With this epiphany, my respect for him grew, and our relationship was formed. I now completely understood anything he dished out was for my good and for the sake of the team. No matter how difficult the practice, I was convinced the purpose of all of his corrections was for my benefit. Consequently,

I became open to all he had in store for me. Looking back, I now realize my personal experience is an illustration of a classic maxim that was one of Coach Wooden's favorites to quote: *"They won't care how much you know until they know how much you care."*

The Relationship Grows

For the rest of the season, our relationship continued to grow. Although still behind Walton in skills, I was catching up and getting closer to the goal that Coach and I had agreed upon—to give Walton all he could handle in practice by progressing as a player myself. A personally gratifying part of Coach's challenges was predicting when he was going to give me something new to master. It was easy. Each time I mastered a skill, concept, or move, he was always there to provide a new one.

But simply demanding more from students makes little sense unless the teacher provides the instruction needed to achieve those high expectations. Teachers need to know enough about each individual that they can adjust their expectations so that they are challenging but not overwhelming. Teachers need to know how much and what kind of emotional support an individual needs to sustain effort in the face of challenging expectations. This is something else Coach Wooden practiced—getting to know his students well enough that he knew what they needed to excel, and using that knowledge to tailor instruction and support for each individual. Combined with high expectations, knowing each student's instructional and emotional needs created the foundation of the enduring teacher-student relationships that he was able to build.

Focused as he was on correcting every mistake I made, the reality was Coach Wooden's attention was primarily directed at those who were going to play in the games. Although he did provide me with feedback during practice sessions, it was his usual practice to correct the regular players, even when I out-maneuvered one of them. Time would not allow him to pay equal attention to both groups.

Not long after the completion of my second UCLA season, I received word that Coach wanted to speak with me. I immediately headed for his office, where he gave me wonderful news. He had arranged for me, a backup center, to receive an invitation to the Olympic trials that summer at the Air Force Academy in Colorado Springs, Colorado.

As I sat there in Coach's office trying to comprehend this exciting news, my thoughts quickly turned to the looming challenge. I would be competing with the best college players in the country. Frankly, it was a frightening and intimidating prospect. Coach must have sensed my rising self-doubts, and what he told me next was partially responsible for me leading all Olympic training camp participants in scoring. He said, *"I wouldn't have asked you if I didn't know you would do well."* At the trials, not one drill, scrimmage, or game ever passed without me thinking of those words. Just as Coach had predicted, I was successful, leading the camp players in scoring and making the team. Unfortunately, during pre-Olympic training, I became ill and had to give my spot to the first alternate.

That next fall, at the first UCLA practice, I was ready to show my teacher that I had reached our goal. After an undefeated season and another NCAA championship, Walton, more than ever, needed to be pushed not only to avoid a letdown, but to continue his development. I was ready to challenge him every day.

Preseason practices were as usual. No matter how diligently we worked on our conditioning prior to the beginning of preseason practices, it didn't matter—our physical conditioning was going to be greatly challenged by Coach.

I had a great preseason and believed I was fulfilling my role on the team. On some days I was more than holding my own against Walton during scrimmages. I was doing so well that I began to think I might receive a little more playing time. I thought that perhaps Coach would be able to take Walton out of games one or two minutes earlier that year. But that didn't happen.

Walton's knees were giving him even more problems than the previous year, and once he headed to the bench and cooled down, his ailing knees would stiffen and wouldn't allow him to return to the court. That meant he had to remain in the game until Coach decided a win was certain. So, during the first half of the season, I received few minutes. Midway through the season, discouragement once again set in. After working so hard every day in practice for two and half years, I began to look ahead to the end of the season and a chance to play professional basketball. The consequences were predictable. My work ethic diminished and, as a result, my level of performance in practice suffered.

After several steps backwards, I decided I wasn't going to let that continue. The next practice session, I arrived 10 minutes early to talk with Coach Wooden. I apologized for the lack of effort and promised him, "For the remainder of the season, no one will outwork me in practice. I'm not asking for playing time, I'm just making a promise." He responded with a smile, a pat on the back and said, *"We'll see."*

Well, he did see: a metamorphosis. In the weeks that followed, there were times I dominated practice. Walton had improved tremendously since first arriving at UCLA, but so had I. On one occasion, after grabbing my fourth offensive rebound in succession, I noticed Coach smiling on the sideline and shouting, *"Well done, Swen."* For the first time in three years, instead of heading directly to the defensive basket, I took a detour toward the sideline where Coach was standing, reached out my open hand as I ran by, and he gave me five. That was a rare occurrence.

For the remainder of the regular season, I was rewarded by being UCLA's first reserve to come off the bench, substituting for either Walton or Keith Wilkes. Toward the end of the season, a reporter asked Walton, "Who is the toughest center you have played against all year?" He immediately responded, "The man I play against every day in practice—Swen Nater." My college career ended in 1973 when UCLA won its seventh NCAA championship in a row, and ninth in 10 years.

The season was over, and practices ended. My lessons in Coach Wooden's classroom had ended. Although I never had the opportunity to play as much as I wanted at UCLA, I was confident I had learned a great deal. My self-satisfaction was confirmed shortly after our season ended when I received word that Coach wanted to talk to me. He had gotten me on the Western Team of the Pizza Hut College All-Star Game, where all of the best college seniors would be showcasing their talents in front of professional scouts. He said that although I didn't receive much playing time during my career at UCLA, he believed I was ready for this challenge and could do well. Just as I had done in the Olympic trials the summer before, I again proved Coach Wooden's confidence in me was justified. I was the MVP of the all-star game. Later that spring, I was chosen in the first round of the NBA Draft. My teacher had taught me well.

They are all Different

Setting high but achievable expectations for students and then identifying what instruction they require is a continuing challenge all teachers face. The same expectations and identical instruction will not work because students differ in many ways. Coach Wooden learned this when he began teaching high school English in the 1930s and made addressing individual differences a cornerstone of his approach throughout his teaching and coaching career.

For example, the 1964 and 1965 championship teams had two starting guards that played together well and were largely responsible for the team's scoring. Gail Goodrich was a left-handed 6-footer who had extremely good hands and long arms, making him a great contributor on the full-court press as well. Goodrich was a good shooter when he was open, but then again, he always thought he was open. Walt Hazzard had a 6-foot-4 strong body and was powerful when he drove to the basket. Goodrich played pure fundamental basketball while Hazzard got fancy every now and then, throwing a behind-the-back pass that sometimes resulted in him warming the seat next to Coach Wooden for a spell.

Giving each of these players different basketball instructions was a given, but in the process, especially in the area of correcting errors made in practice, Coach Wooden approached each with a different style. *"With Gail, I had to be very careful. Language too strong would have caused him to go into his shell. A*

UCLA coach John Wooden faced very different challenges in teaching reserve center Swen Nater (left) and All-American center Bill Walton (right).

pat on the back worked well for Gail. But, with the confidence Walt had, if I patted him on the back too much, it would have gone to his head."[4]

To deal with individual differences, Wooden imposed on himself a high expectation: Closely monitor each individual's progress, study the inner workings of each, and teach and respond accordingly. He began this practice in the 1930s when he was a high school teacher, long before the research community had begun to study the impact of setting expectations and constantly monitoring individual performance. With a goal of delivering exactly the right instruction at the right time to each student—so that motivation and progress would spawn confidence and initiative—Coach Wooden began experimenting to determine what strategies worked best. His observational persistence paid off, and this became a permanent part of his teaching repertoire: Continuously monitoring the progress of each individual in order to tailor instruction to be the most effective. During practices, he and his assistants kept a supply of 3 x 5 index cards and recorded observations for each individual.

"By doing that I could track the practice routines of every single player for every single practice session he participated in while I was coaching him. ... It was very important that I learn about each player and then study that player so I would know if he needed a little more time on this or that particular drill. I needed to know which drill had greater application to this player or that player, because individuals vary. So I devised drills for both individuals and the group and studied and analyzed them. Some drills would be good for all and some drills would be good for just certain players."[5]

For example, during Coach Wooden's final season as UCLA's coach, a young center was struggling to learn the finer points of his position. After taking a defensive rebound, the young player often hesitated before making the pass. Whenever he hesitated, Coach Wooden always corrected him with a short, concise instruction. One time after the young man got the rebound, he hesitated instead of making the outlet pass to start the fast break, and Coach shouted, *"Pass the ball to someone short!"[6]* That crisp, timely correction was the direct product of the "lesson plan" developed that morning for this individual. Coach was ready with a concise instruction when he saw the young center start to dribble. He knew that day on the practice court that he would be looking for opportunities to teach the young center a key skill. He also had other teaching goals that day for the young man, and for every other individual on the team.

Beginning with his high school English classes, Coach Wooden conducted the same type of research on his students. Although his English students were enrolled, not recruited, he sought out (without being nosy) information about each of them. His sources were former teachers, parents and other family members (but not siblings), others, and his own observations. The result was teaching with a very personal touch.

Years after I left UCLA as a student and player, I had the opportunity to ask Coach Wooden how he learned so much about me. He responded, *"From you. I learned from you. I watched you, listened to you, and studied you because I cared about helping you reach your potential."*

"What did you learn from me, Coach?" I asked. "What did I teach you?"

"Although every student is different, I had prior experience with a few players who were very much like you. This helped me when I began to work with you because, what worked with them, I tried on you. I learned how you responded to instruction. I watched carefully how you interacted with your teammates, how you got along with others, what frustrated you, and how much pressure I could put on you. I learned, among other things, that you were a very sensitive young man and that a gentle word of encouragement went a lot further than a scold. And yet, I learned, the more I demanded from you, the more you wanted."[8]

I was flattered, even though I knew, in his investigation, he surely found many things not very flattering. But, nonetheless, I was pleased that he would care that much about me and each of his other students. It also helps explain why I felt he understood and cared about me in that life-altering meeting I had with him after my first days of practice at UCLA. He did know who I was, and he did understand what made me tick. He knew me perhaps better than I knew myself.

But there are more benefits from gathering information about students than simply allowing teachers to adjust an individual's instruction. Those who get to know students well become not only expert detectives but better teachers. The more they learn about each student, the more they will learn about all their students. This approach helps a teacher connect new ideas to each individual, and provide the instruction and treatment each individual needs and deserves. Although the task of gathering information about students is arduous, the benefits are priceless. Once it becomes a standard practice, teachers say, "I don't know how I ever taught without this kind of knowledge!" They also discover it is a powerful means to building effective teacher-student relationships.

Respect and Fairness

Teachers face a daunting challenge. Enforcing high expectations and correcting errors are not necessarily going to endear students to the teacher. All of us have had tough teachers who might have known their subject matter, but were not very well liked. They might have taught what we needed to know, but we might not have developed the warm relationship that so many former students have with Coach Wooden. But there were two constants in Coach Wooden's approach to his students and others that were the key to the strong, enduring relationships he has with so many people: Treating others with respect and fairness.

Treating others with respect was not a "technique" he used to build winning teams, it was the expression of a fundamental value he honored. Those who know Coach marvel at his respect for everyone he knows and meets, no matter how celebrated or humble. It is revealed in every interaction he has with another person. One of the most telling examples was his attitude and behavior toward custodians at the universities where UCLA played road games. Custodians are responsible for cleaning the visiting locker rooms after they have been vacated. Coach explicitly taught his teams to leave their locker room as clean as they found it, and we did. Apparently, not every visiting team practiced equal consideration, because the custodians were particularly impressed with our standard practice. Not only were they impressed, but some of them expressed their appreciation by writing Coach Wooden letters to that effect. On a couple of occasions he read to us, with obvious satisfaction, excerpts from those letters.

The value of each human life, no matter how humble or celebrated, was taught by his father, Joshua Wooden, who told a very young John Wooden that no one is better than you and you are not better than anyone else.

Coach Wooden is also a stickler for fairness. But for him, that did not mean treating all of his players and students exactly alike. In the 1930s, he came up with an approach he calls "earned and deserved." *"I believe, in order to be fair to all students, a teacher must give each individual student the treatment he earns and deserves. The most unfair thing to do is to treat all of them the same."*

As his students on the basketball court at UCLA, we quickly learned how this system worked. During our preseason team meeting every year, Coach made it a point to say this:

"I am not going to treat you players all the same. Giving you the same treatment does not make sense because you're all different. The good Lord, in his infinite wisdom, did not make us all the same. Goodness gracious, if he had, this would be a boring world, don't you think? You are different from each other in height, weight, background, intelligence, talent, and many other ways. For that reason, each one of you deserves individual treatment that is best for you. I will decide what that treatment will be. It may take the form of gentle encouragement or something a little stronger. That depends on you. It may also take the form of discipline. But remember, all discipline will be earned by you based on what you have done prior. So, I'm not going to treat you all the same, but I will give you the treatment you earn and deserve."[10]

Coach Wooden didn't just make that speech the first day and then not follow through on his words. Whether it was allowing a player to eat a different pre-game meal or wear different sneakers than the rest of his teammates, he carefully considered individual treatment, all the while keeping in mind the effect it would have on the team.

"*The pre-game meal menu was the same for every player: New York steak, baked potato with one slice of butter, Melba toast, and a cup of mixed fruit. However, Lew Alcindor (later known as Kareem Abdul-Jabbar), asked me if he could pass on such a heavy meal, eat some fruit and have his steak after the game when all of us would eat together again. I understood his reason and granted him his wish. Interestingly, no other player ever asked for the same treatment, perhaps because, after the game, they could order anything they wanted and hamburgers were a popular choice.*

"*Sidney Wicks and Curtis Rowe, probably the two best forwards in the country, were very good examples to the rest. However, on one occasion, they were seven minutes late to a pre-game meal. I didn't say a word, expecting them to come and give me their excuses. They never did. For that reason, they didn't play the first seven minutes of that evening's game, and it was a very important conference game. Had any one of them given me the reason for their tardiness I would have allowed them to play, provided the excuse was valid. The reason is they had earned it. Players who had records of violations may not have been granted the same, but would certainly have received the treatment they earned and deserved.*

"*Henry Bibby, a brilliant sharp-shooting guard, asked to be allowed to wear a different brand of shoe, Pro Keds. For the purpose of uniformity, I pre-ferred all my players wore the same brand. But I allowed Henry to change because he had extremely flat feet and the Pro Keds seemed to be more con-ducive to the form of his foot. Had another player asked the same favor, and I knew it was for fashion purposes, I would have denied the request.*"[11]

Perhaps the concept of "earned and deserved" can be best understood with an example of one of Coach Wooden's "rules"—the rule for tardiness. All of us were very clear on what we were to do should we be tardy. We were to come to the practice floor, dressed in our school clothes, and give Coach our excuse. If he deemed it a worthy excuse and we had a relatively clean record of viola-tions, we would be allowed to go to the dressing room, get dressed for prac-tice, and join the team. If he didn't believe the excuse was justified, we would be held out of practice for that day. Practice was a privilege and though it was extremely taxing, no one wanted to miss out. For the reserves it was fun because we got to play against the best. For the regular players, missing one practice might result in a loss of playing time, and repeated offenses might result in expulsion from the team. Needless to say, UCLA did not have a tar-diness problem.

Coach Wooden's rule on tardiness—that he had the *option* to dismiss us from practice, with each situation and player judged differently—was a clear statement of his reasoning. It was obvious he had wisely thought out this particular method of working with his students and that he believed it was the fairest way. Although some players may not have agreed with all of Coach's decisions, we had no doubt he was being fair. We all liked this system and preferred it to one in which rules and consequences were presented at the beginning of the season and, no matter who you were or what you had done, the rule determined what the consequences were to be.

"Earned and deserved" was not solely designed for discipline. As mentioned in the examples above, each student earned special treatment by what he did and deserved special treatment by who he was. Coach Wooden's players earned credit, if you will, by being considerate of the team and the coaching staff, and they deserved tailor-made treatment in order to progress in skill and confidence.

How is Coach Wooden's "earned and deserved" approach different from standard practice? A good example is a story told by a young high school football coach who was beginning his second year. He had inherited a successful program, which was picked to be number one in the state, but his team ended that season by losing in the championship game. But it was a decision the coach made prior to the game that may have ultimately decided the game's outcome.

Away from home and in a different corner of the state, his players were housed in a hotel on the eve of the championship game. As with any team of young men, rules had to be established. One of those rules was a curfew of 11 p.m. the night before the championship game. The rule applied to all, and any violation, regardless of the player or the excuse, would result in a spot on the sideline for the championship game. What the young coach least expected was that his star running back—the team's leading scorer—was five minutes late returning to the hotel. Leaving his wallet at a restaurant, the running back went back to retrieve it. It was the first time this young man had violated a rule in four years and his track record would have revealed a consistent demonstration of cooperation and respect for the rules. But the coach felt he had no recourse but to follow through with the consequences. Without its leading scorer, the team lost a game it most likely would have won. In his effort to be fair, the coach had made a mistake—he didn't understand the most unfair thing to do is to treat everyone the same.

Relationships are the Ends, Not the Means

Now, many years after my college days, I have developed a routine of arriving early at airports. Once there, I find a place to read until the boarding call. On one occasion, deeply engrossed, I almost didn't hear the question, "Are you Swen Nater?" as someone approached me, recognizing me from my playing days, which happens frequently.

The conversations are always about basketball and frequently turn to the subject of my college basketball coach, John Wooden. This instance was no exception. The gentleman asked a question I've heard a thousand times: "John Wooden seems like such a nice man. I bet it was a pleasure playing for him, wasn't it?" What an opportunity it was for me to reveal a little known but wonderful quality of my teacher.

I responded this way: "From the moment he stepped on the practice floor, he set the tone for the intensity; the meter was always pegged high, and he worked our tails off for the entire two hours. He demanded our best effort, every minute of practice. He corrected every mistake, became disgusted and impatient often, and sparingly distributed praises. Mentally, emotionally, and physically, he drove us to the brink of collapse. It seemed like nothing was ever good enough. Perfection was what he was after. He was like a drill sergeant.

"And he didn't stop there. He demanded impeccable class attendance, never condoned inconsiderate treatment of others, strongly addressed waste, despised the mistreatment of animals, and would not put up with inappropriate language. If he found one piece of trash in our locker room after a practice, we would hear about it at his next opportunity. He was a stickler for proper dress; even our practice shirts were to be tucked in with a minimum degree of slack allowed. Any player who tried to get away with anything was immediately spotted and received a lecture."

The gentleman was shocked. "I had no idea John Wooden was like that. I always thought you guys liked him."

"But we do!" I replied emphatically. "We love him. We loved him then and we love him now. I don't know how to explain it, but it's true."

A survey of coaches and teachers across this country would reveal that some are demanding, some extremely tough, some fair, and some individualize instruction and treatment for their students. Some manage to blend high expectations, continuous assessment of students, and unfailing interest, care, respect, and fairness to build "learning partnerships" with their students. Such a partnership is a close relationship, in which both teacher and student work equally as hard, with mutual respect keeping the relationship strong.

But these "learning partnerships" were not the beginning steps; they were a product of something more fundamental. In my case, Coach Wooden never overtly tried to develop a close relationship during my first year at UCLA. The relationship was born in his commitment to and steadfastness in teaching me, in responding to my concerns, and in careful tracking of my progress. Our relationship was forged slowly over time, and strengthened by the combination of the intense fire of his high expectations and my determination to learn. It matured when it became a "learning relationship" and my respect for him caught up with his respect for me.

Coach Wooden won a record 10 NCAA national championships, including seven in a row, with both Nater and Walton helping the Bruins win the 1972 national title.

These ideas can be applied to good use by teachers and school administrators. Rather than beginning with relationship building, relationships evolve out of getting something done that everyone agrees is important to accomplish.[12] This same dynamic is seen many times in schools that are facing hardships and challenges. Productive relationships and powerful learning communities are found in those situations where teachers and administrators set realistic goals to work toward, track their progress, and don't give up until they have found a way to help students learn better. It sounds so simple, and in some ways it is, but it is very difficult to do—just as it was difficult for Coach Wooden to win championships with so many different combinations of players and talent levels over the course of a 47-year career. But it works.

My personal experience confirms the effectiveness of Coach Wooden's principles and practices. In the history of professional basketball, no one who had failed to play high school basketball or start in a major college basketball game was ever drafted in the first round of the NBA and ABA until I was fortunate enough to be chosen. I was named the 1974 ABA Rookie of the Year, and in various years throughout my career led the ABA, NBA, and Italian League in rebounding. At UCLA, I was a practice player, but I went on to play 12 years of professional basketball, mostly as a starter. My teacher's prophecy was accurate. Come to UCLA and you will learn to be the best you can be, if you are willing to put in the effort to learn.

The challenge Coach Wooden faced to keep me engaged and to maintain a relationship with me was not his first such challenge. During his 27 years at UCLA, he dealt with many complex relationship issues in his classroom. His autobiography and various other books about him recount many instances in which he built and maintained positive relationships with players who did not begin their college careers very well, or who encountered difficulties during their time at UCLA.

Not every player responded as I did to the constant corrections that were routine in Coach Wooden's classroom on the court. The circumstances in the school classroom might be different in many ways, but in others they are identical to the practice court. Although there were few, when some UCLA players began to realize they would never get to play much, their motivation to learn and work hard in practice diminished. They felt there was little point in trying hard in practice if success, as they defined it, was beyond reach, so they left UCLA. But in most cases, Coach Wooden's approach succeeded: Setting challenging expectations appropriate to each individual; getting to know each individual well and caring for each as a person; tailoring his instructions and support to individual differences; and treating everyone with respect and fairness. It succeeded for him in the classroom, on the court, and in life.

Success

Some say success is in fortune and fame,
Or winning the crown in a championship game.
Some say success is in riches and gold,
Or trophies and medals—That's what we've been told.

We worship the winners who shine in the race,
And shame all the trailers who hold second place.
We train our poor children to only be best.
"Success is just when you're ahead of the rest."

We tell them success is an A or a B,
And that something is wrong if they bring home a C.
"What's wrong with the teacher?
Why can't my child pass?
My child's name should be at the top of the class.

My taxes are spent and remain in their pay,
So why is my genius not getting an A?
My child is not average," They say as they're riled.
"That place is reserved for the neighborhood child."

But God in His wisdom, when making this race,
Did not make us equal in talent and grace.
For some of us run, but then others are lame.
But both share success if they try just the same.

If you came up short when you went for the A,
But gave it your all till the very last day,
And effort was made to be all you can be,
You're still a success if you brought home a C.

When you know that you gave it all, then you'll find,
That self-satisfaction gives sweet peace of mind.
And that peace of mind, that you only possess,
Is your declaration that you're a success.

Swen Nater

Chapter 2

The Motivation to Learn Comes from Focusing on Reaching Your Own Potential

Just like all teachers, John Wooden had many students who were never going to be at the top of their class. They might spend most if not all of their UCLA careers as reserves. They were never going to start, see their exploits described in print, or see themselves on TV replays. I was not the only member of a UCLA basketball team to have that experience. Many who played for Coach Wooden have reported similar experiences.[1] One of the major reasons was his emphasis on team play.

"I wanted the players to understand that I'm only going to play seven, probably never over eight. And my players have to learn to accept that. ... I feel that we got better continuity [playing a limited number]. [Those that played regularly were] far more accustomed to playing together than if I was making constant substitutions. I wanted the regulars to have a lot of time working together so they'd learn to know each other on the floor."[2]

When I joined the UCLA team, at first I thought I sensed equal opportunity. But that feeling did not last long. My more talented and experienced teammates became "regulars," while the rest of us became members of the supporting cast—the reserves. It all seemed depressingly similar to my experiences in elementary school, shortly after my family emigrated from the Netherlands to the United States. Each fall I would start out certain that this would be the year I would become one of the "academic stars" of the class. But after a few weeks, each student was ranked, or self-labeled, to a position that rarely changed for the rest of the school year. Every year my hopes were dashed. It was very discouraging. What was I to do? How was I going to maneuver my way up the academic status ladder? If I could just get the teacher's attention; if I could find a way to please my teacher, make my teacher happy, smile, or be impressed with something. I would spend the rest of the year coming to school early, doing extra credit, and asking lots of questions. When my teacher was pleased, I was motivated to keep trying. When my teacher wasn't, I became discouraged.

But my UCLA basketball teacher was different than most of my previous instructors. Coach Wooden held "non-stars"—the reserves—in high esteem. He managed to kindle motivation for personal success of a kind and intensity I had never before experienced. He believed that for the team to be successful, everyone—starters and reserves alike—had to be motivated to work hard in practice so that the starting players could be challenged and improve. For this to work, it was crucial to keep the reserves motivated by stressing the importance of their contributions to the team.

"The [reserves] are going to be needed, [and I needed to let them know that]. You're going to be developing those that are going to be playing the most and you're very important ... we may have an injury or a sickness or some other thing that might cause us to lose one of [the regulars]. You have to be ready to step in. If the reserves are dogging it there's not going to be any improvement in the regulars. So, I've got to constantly get across to them how much they are needed. I think it took a special effort to make sure that we do have harmony on the group as a whole."[3]

To accomplish this, Coach Wooden made the igniting of individual motivation a central teaching principle for all his students, even those who might be intimidated or discouraged by the success of more talented peers. How he did that grew from his experiences as a young teacher. What he developed, he believes works in classrooms just as well as it does on the practice court.

In 1932, when he began teaching in high school, Coach Wooden quickly realized that students demonstrated very different gifts. Some became frustrated and discouraged if they received anything less than an A or B. He did not have the authority to eliminate grades and yet he wondered how to define success in a way that would motivate everyone to learn. Like in so many other areas of his life, Coach turned to his roots for inspiration. What emerged eventually became a successful way to motivate every student and player—even those who never believed they were going to become stars.

John Wooden's Definition of Success

His father, Joshua Wooden, had repeatedly stressed he should never try to be better than someone else, but that he should never cease to try and become the best that he could be. Echoing his father's wisdom were other sources, such as George Mariority's poem, which says in part,

Coach Wooden doesn't define success by wins and losses, but rather by the effort made to become the best of which you are capable.

"For who can ask more of a man, than giving all within his span?
Giving all, it seems to me, is not so far from victory."

Reflecting on many sources, Wooden settled on the following definition, which he felt clearly communicated his father's ideas and practices:

"Success is the peace of mind which is a direct result of the self-satisfaction in knowing that you have made the effort to become the best of which you are capable."

For Coach, the definition made sense, not only for talented and gifted students, but for everyone else as well. If all students could be convinced to concentrate on their own progress, every individual should gain and maintain motivation. In other words, if he could somehow get them to think of passing to a higher level of achievement instead of passing another student, they would immediately see the next level of knowledge and go for it. If the reward for hard work was moving ahead, even if it's just little steps, that could be motivating.

Coach Wooden knew the concept to be well founded, for he had seen it work in his own life. As a high school and college student, he had stopped comparing himself to other students and athletes, and chose to focus on making the effort to become the best he could. It worked. At one point in his basketball career at Purdue University, he was considered to be the best basketball player in the country and was rewarded by being named an All-American for three straight years.

He also applied the same approach to academics at Purdue, focusing on constantly improving his learning and achievement. He succeeded so well in the classroom that it resulted in what he calls his most prized award—being awarded the Big Ten Conference medal for outstanding achievement in academics in 1932. While Coach Wooden cherishes that award, he says he did not work hard on his academics to earn any reward beyond the satisfaction of knowing he had made the best effort as a student of which he was capable.

When he began teaching and coaching, his definition of success continued to play a vital role in his approach to students. The following comments are typical of the many people whom he taught or coached:

"He drove everybody, but with a conception that always had value: Make yourself as good as you can be," Pete Blackman said. "Always. There was very little emphasis on the opposition ... very little attempt to understand what they were going to do on the theory that if you do the best you can, you're going to statistically come out well. These are lessons of a profound nature. Focus on yourself, your own values, doing things correctly."[4]

"The pre-game speech was not, 'You have to run over them ...'" Walt Hazzard said. "It was, 'At the end of the game, everyone here should be capable of walking to the mirror and looking at themselves, and saying to themselves, I did the best I could.'"[5]

The Old Man with Wooden Clubs

'Twas a Saturday sunrise and three of us friends,
Were waiting upon the first tee.
We were crowned in the latest of golfing attire,
Imperially well-draped were we.

Titanium drivers, new irons that gleamed,
And golf balls, the top-of-the-line.
Our shoes bore the labels of recognized brands,
And they glittered like gold from the shine.

When, out of the clubhouse, the manager came,
And said with a courteous smile,
"I've added a fourth who will join you today,
Though he doesn't come close to your style."

His clothes were in season three decades ago,
And he looked like he came from the past.
A faded old cap and his faded old shoes,
Were, to ours, a striking contrast.

But his most antiquated component was this:
The wooden-shaft clubs that he bore.
They were battered and dented and seemed to belong,
In the back of a second-hand store.

While the three of us stepped to the tee in our turn,
And we drove all three balls down the way,
And they sailed and they landed a fair distance out,
The man chose the club he would play.

With care and respect, he lifted the stick,
And wisely considered the breeze.
He looked down the fairway, and addressed the ball,
And his swing had a grace and an ease.

His ball started low and began to ascend,
And it rose like a kite in the air.
It went straight like an arrow and landed well-past,
The three other balls that were there.

Our second shots scattered somewhere near the green,
And the old man took out an old wedge.
When he struck it, the ball seemed to search for the hole,
And it landed three feet from its edge.

He birdied and I looked at him, while I thought,
That his luck was absurd and bizarre.
But we bogeyed hole two as we watched the old man,
Sink a twenty-foot putt for a par.

And so it persisted for sixteen more holes,
He continued to give us our licks,
And he did it with skill and humility's grace,
And with antique and battered old sticks.

At the end of the round, as the handshakes commenced,
I asked him, for all of us three,
"How could you, an old man with outdated clubs,
Play superior and better than we?"

The stare of his eyes penetrated my soul,
As my heart sensed the wisdom of age,
He spoke, and, for me, what I heard has become,
My yardstick, my compass and gauge.

"Equipment has little to do with the score;
It's the person who's holding the wood.
If he's doing his best with the clubs that he has,
He'll probably be pretty good."

Then I realized how life resembles the game,
That like "top-of-the-line" clubs and ball,
Some, when they're born, have a silvery spoon,
But then others have no spoons at all.

Possessions have little to do with success,
It's the person who's holding his share.
If he's doing his best with whatever he's got,
He'll probably be pretty fair.

                    Swen Nater

The Pyramid of Success

Coach Wooden soon discovered that a definition of success alone was not sufficient to motivate his students. They needed a road map with reachable milestones (short-term goals) along the way. Moderately difficult goals, when reached, result in a sense of self-accomplishment and motivation to immediately continue toward the next short-term goal. Each time a milestone is reached, a sense of self-satisfaction is generated and motivation to continue is fueled. Satisfied with his definition of success, Coach began to look for a "curriculum," which included attainable milestones to keep his students focused on self-evaluation, rather than external rewards. He ran across a few interesting systems, one of which was a ladder of achievement. At the top of the ladder was the word, "Success." On each rung of the ladder a character trait was written, such as "hard work" or "integrity." He liked the idea and began designing his own structure. After identifying all the components he thought were important, a pyramid consisting of blocks began to emerge.

In 1932, the Pyramid of Success was completed and the structure has essentially not been altered, although a block or two has been moved to an alternate position. With his definition of success at the top, the structure consists of 15 blocks and several additional traits placed on the outside of each side of the triangle. Comparing Coach Wooden's system for motivation to a trip from Los Angeles to New York, the definition states the destination (New York) while the milestones are cities along the way, such as Phoenix, Albuquerque, Denver, Chicago, and Detroit. Each block in the Pyramid of Success is a milestone, providing students/players with a succession of achievable goals.

Over the years, Coach Wooden has presented the Pyramid of Success to literally thousands of audiences. He speaks without notes, with humor, and in an understated tone. Whatever the nature or size of the audience, the presentation begins with a brief history of the Pyramid, the definition, and proceeds one block at a time. Each block is defined and illustrated with sometimes humorous, tragic, or shining examples from his long career of teaching, coaching, and leading by example.

The typical response from audiences is at once electric and hushed. Picture a man in his 90s, sitting in front of 200 UCLA undergraduates, with his cane lying on the floor. Are the students really interested? Oh, yes. As the hour-long presentation proceeds, block by block, there is a connection across the generations that is magical. His ability to captivate audiences of various ages and generations impresses everyone who has witnessed it.

It would be easy to assume that as much emphasis as Coach Wooden places on the Pyramid, his players must have memorized the blocks and their embedded values. But that isn't the case. Here are some comments from former UCLA players about how Coach used the Pyramid:

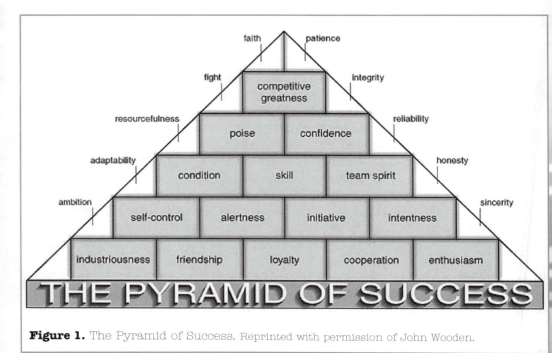

Figure 1. The Pyramid of Success. Reprinted with permission of John Wooden.

"He used to have the Pyramid of Success on his desk and on his wall, also," Denny Crum said. "I knew about it as a player because it was right there in his office, but he didn't push it on us."[6]

"... He never proselytizes about anything," Kareem Abdul-Jabbar said. "He would try to get you to read the Pyramid of Success, but that was about all."[7]

"Wooden never presented the Pyramid to anybody, saying, 'You should be this way,' or 'You have to be this way to meet my needs,'" Dr. John Berberich said. "He just lived it that way."[8]

Coach Wooden learned early in his career that giving each of his players a "manual" to study was not the way to convey his ideas.[9] Instead, he fused the values in the blocks of the Pyramid into his words and deeds so that they were part of his everyday interactions with players and anyone else with whom he came into contact. From time to time he posted some of his Pyramid-related maxims on a bulletin board. When he spoke with individual players, these values guided his advice and comments. On the practice floor, he salted the many corrections with short reminders of his values.

The ones he stressed the most were industriousness, enthusiasm, condition, skill, and team spirit. Coach Wooden was successful in integrating these five blocks of the Pyramid into his teaching and into his players' very fiber. This helped his players move toward ultimate success—not the cheers from the fans or the championship banners, but "*peace of mind which is a direct result of the self-satisfaction in knowing that you have made the effort to become the best of which you are capable."*

Industriousness and Enthusiasm

Industriousness (hard work) and enthusiasm (a genuine love for what you are doing) are the cornerstones for success. Some people work very hard, but they will lose their drive if they don't care about what they're engaged in. Others may have a fervent love for what they are doing, but lack the character to work as hard as needed and to sustain that work. Both qualities are needed in order to achieve success.

The majority of Coach Wooden's players probably had no problem loving the game of basketball. It was our passion. But when the squad was divided into the regulars and reserves, enthusiasm diminished for some of us. How did Coach keep reserve players enthusiastic? It was probably his most difficult assignment.

I played about three minutes a game during my junior year. The following summer I had worked hard and made the Olympic basketball team. Not only did I make it, but I led the entire training camp in scoring. I surprised everyone in the nation because I was a bench warmer at UCLA, so no one had any idea of how talented I was. I didn't know either. Instantly, I achieved national visibility and became, in the eyes of professional scouts, a potential first-round draft choice.

But, when my senior year commenced, and practice started, it was business as usual. I was a reserve and playing time was limited to the last three minutes of a game, when the outcome had already been determined. But I knew Coach Wooden was looking for a way to get me more time. I had earned it.

For almost the entire season, I worked as hard, or harder, than anyone else. I never forgot the words Coach Wooden said during the preseason meeting. "You reserves should always be thinking, 'I will get myself ready and then my chance may come.'" Believing his words, I worked hard to prepare myself for my opportunity.

Although my job was to help develop Bill Walton, Coach continued to pay almost as much attention to me as he did to Walton. He corrected me (a million times, I'm sure), encouraged me, drove me, challenged me, and got impatient with me. Had he ignored me because of my "reserve status," I would probably have given up hope. But he didn't ignore me at all, not even once, as the following incident reveals.

During a road game in Pullman, Washington, near the end of league play, the contest had been decided and I entered the game with two minutes to play. Two minutes. That's not even enough time to get tired! One of the Cougars missed a shot and I grabbed the rebound. Andy Hill, one of my teammates, quickly cut to the corner to receive my outlet pass. It was just as we practiced.

My pass to him would start the fast break to the other end of the court. But a strange thought entered my head. "If I pass Andy the ball, I'll probably (no, certainly) not see it again." So I decided to keep the ball and dribble down the court like a guard. What did I have to lose?

Now, it's important to know this game was on national television, for even today, fans from all over the country remind me of what happened next. From the UCLA bench seat, closest to the scorer's table, Coach Wooden yelled (and the microphones easily picked it up), "Swen, you are not to dribble the ball!"

I passed the ball to Hill. The important thing, however, is that Coach Wooden's exhortation clearly communicated how much he cared about my development. He was interested in me enough that even in a game long decided in our favor he would not pass up a chance to correct my play even during "garbage time." He did not let a single error pass, no matter how inconsequential it may have seemed to others.

It was this kind of unrelenting focus on my improvement that helped me give maximum effort during practice sessions. Eventually, I got my chance to be a regular. I became the first or second man off the bench for the remaining regular season games. It was Coach Wooden's attention that kept me enthusiastic about basketball and motivated me to work hard. He said my extra playing time was earned and deserved.

During practice sessions, his attention took the form of constant recognition of small improvements, especially in the areas of hard work and enthusiasm, and by doing so helped me notice my own improvement. During the last few weeks of the season, as I worked as hard, or harder, than my teammates, Coach occasionally made reference to my renewed love for the game and improved industriousness. But I noticed it also. The harder I worked, the better I became, and the better I became, the harder I wanted to work.

But this was the end of a process, which began when I accepted Coach's maxim that success comes from working as hard as you can to be the best you can be, without comparing yourself to the accomplishments of others. Compared to Walton, I was not successful. Few would have been. But by practicing Coach's definition, personal success was all up to me.

The Heart of the Pyramid

Condition, skill, and team spirit are the heart of the Pyramid of Success. It makes sense, doesn't it? One has to be conditioned to be at one's best when best is needed. The execution of the fundamentals must become automatic and each player must be eagerly committed to performing his role for the benefit of the team.

Steady improvement in several areas continued to provide me with motivation to reach my personal best, but nothing motivated me more than enhanced conditioning, skill, and team spirit. The better my conditioning, the harder I could work to improve my skills. The better my skills, the better I could give them to the team. As all three were improving simultaneously, I could literally see daily improvement. It was exciting. I felt good about myself.

1. Condition

For basketball, condition means moral, mental, and physical conditioning. Being in physical shape, we all understood; we had all been conditioned each year we played basketball. But we never heard about "moral and mental conditioning."

Moral Conditioning

UCLA basketball players were not exempt from normal college temptations. Staying up late, drinking alcohol, partying, and not studying were all easy to succumb to if we were not careful. At the end of almost every practice session, Coach Wooden reminded us, *"Now you boys are working hard to get in physical condition—all of you. But you can throw it all away by what you do between prac-*

Courtesy of Purdue University Sports Information
As a player at Purdue University from 1930-32, John Wooden was viewed as one of the best in the nation, earning All-American honors for three straight seasons.

tices. *On the other hand, if you take care of yourself by getting the proper rest and taking care of your bodies, you'll end up in the best condition you can be.*" Believe it or not, we listened. I could feel the benefits of avoiding parties, eating properly, and getting the right hours of sleep (not just the amount of hours but the same hours each night). The improvement gave me a euphoric feeling and I wanted more. So, I consumed even better quality food and experimented with the amount of hours of rest I needed to be at my best.

Mental Conditioning

Some of us were incredibly good at keeping our concentration. Others were easily distracted by officials, fans, and other things out of our control. Mental conditioning was pivotal to playing your best. Coach Wooden was extremely impatient with mental errors, especially if the same error was committed twice.

"*Goodness, gracious sakes alive!*" he shouted at one of my teammates when he got the ball stolen two times in a row during a scrimmage. "*Can't you see he has his hand down, covering your cross-over dribble? He's off balance when he reaches. Fake and drive or cross-over closer to your body. How many times does he need to steal it before you learn?*" That was a pretty lengthy statement for Coach. Usually, his corrections were much more economical. But whether short or long, they were always powerful. In a real sense, he was helping us strengthen our minds by creating incredible resistance and pressure. That pressure was intense every practice, all practice long, for the entire season.

For me, his mental pressure meant he cared. It meant he wanted me to continue making progress in the area of mental conditioning. I got used to it and fed off it. When I arrived at UCLA, I was notorious for making the same mistake more than once. But, each time Coach Wooden put the pressure on me, I improved and with each little step of improvement, I wanted more (intrinsic motivation). My goal was to not make the same mistake twice.

2. Skill

Coach Wooden continued to keep our minds off winning and increase our momentum toward personal success. Skill is the quick and proper execution of the fundamentals of basketball. Shooting, rebounding, passing, cutting, and receiving were all basics of the game.

During one of our scrimmages, our team, the reserves, ran a perfect play and one of our forwards received the basketball about 15 feet from the basket, wide open. He was so open, it surprised him, and as a result he hesitated. When he finally shot the ball, it was blocked by a defender. Coach Wooden quickly blew the whistle and approached the player. "*You're a good shooter, but that's not enough. If you're going to be your best, you must learn to shoot, not only properly, but quickly and without thinking. If you have to think about how and when to shoot, you'll miss and you'll shoot too late.*" The next time that player was open, he didn't hesitate to shoot the ball, resulting in a beautifully made basket.

The realization of little steps of improvement in my skill probably motivated me more than anything because there were instant rewards. For example, at one point during my junior year, I learned that keeping my hands up above my shoulders when going for a rebound was very effective. Most rebounds are retrieved below the rim and, before, when I didn't have my hands up, it would bounce right past me. With my newly acquired skill, I probably grabbed 10 more rebounds each practice session. But that wasn't enough for me. I wanted more and more. With my eye on my personal best, I continued to make progress after college. I became the ABA, NBA, and Italian League's leading rebounder during my professional career.

3. Team Spirit

Team spirit was perhaps the most difficult concept for Coach Wooden to get his players to buy into. All of us had been superstars at our previous schools and averaged more than 20 points per game. We were used to the glamour of scoring. Through continued emphasis and recognition of the beauty of a group working for a high-percentage shot, all of us began to see things his way. Making the pass, which led to the pass for a score, became unusually satisfying. Unselfish team play, to Coach, was beautiful, but that did not motivate all UCLA players in the early stages of their playing careers.

Andre McCarter and Pete Trgovich were members of Coach Wooden's last championship team in 1975. Both were high scorers and stars on their high school teams and came to UCLA expecting more of the same. However, what Coach had in mind for those two, in respect to their contribution to the team, did not involve being leading scorers, or even scoring very much at all. He saw

Courtesy of UCLA Photography
The success of Coach Wooden's UCLA teams was directly related to the values embedded in his Pyramid of Success.

both as potentially great defensive players because of their mental and physical quickness.

I remember McCarter's first year. In fact, I remember his first practice. It was my junior year. McCarter entered the floor dribbling between his legs and behind his back. But while I admired his athleticism, I had compassion for him. I knew Coach Wooden would never condone fancy play, and what McCarter was doing was fancy, according to Coach.

It took McCarter until his junior year to realize that Coach Wooden was not going to help him become the nation's leading scorer. Marques Johnson, Richard Washington, and Dave Meyers were all the scorers UCLA needed. To maintain the high level of play that characterized UCLA basketball, defensive guards were extremely important to the system; the guards were responsible for preventing any player from penetrating between them and into the middle of the lane. McCarter had to make a choice. Should he continue to be a "Fancy Dan," as Coach put it, and sit the bench, waiting for a pro contract, or should he buy into Coach's approach, playing the role that the UCLA system required?

Trgovich, a tall guard with long arms, though extremely talented, had not managed to break into the regular lineup for the same reasons as McCarter. As Coach Wooden put it many times to many players, it's a pity these two highly talented players were letting others beat them out of a starting position.

At about the same time in their playing careers, McCarter and Trgovich both chose to accept Coach Wooden's concept of team play. The moment they decided to allow him to teach them to play within the UCLA approach, they began to make enormous strides, and so did the team. The result was, according to Coach, a milestone in his career at UCLA.

"Andre and Pete were the best pair of defensive guards I ever had—not individually necessarily, but they were the best pair. One thing I teach and insist on is not allowing middle dribble penetration. Rarely was any opponent able to split between them."[10]

McCarter and Trgovich were the starting guards on UCLA's 1974-75 team, which surprised basketball experts by winning its 10th national title. It was also the last team Coach Wooden ever guided. He retired after the 1975 national championship game. Trgovich graduated, but McCarter had one more year to play. After McCarter's senior year, he made a plea to Coach to return to campus to attend the graduation ceremonies. After receiving his diploma, McCarter asked, "You never thought I would get this, did you, Coach?"

Coach replied, *"Andre, I didn't think you would last that long."*

"You probably cost me a $1 million dollar professional contract by changing my game," McCarter said, "but I love you more than you'll ever know."

More than 25 years later, Coach Wooden was awarded the Presidential Medal of Freedom in 2003. The man who initiated and led the nomination process was Andre McCarter.

It All Comes Together

I remember a moment when I felt all that I had learned from Coach Wooden about his definition of success and the Pyramid of Success came together. It was during a game late in my final season against Oregon State. Walton was at center and I had entered the game as a strong forward. As we ran our half-court offense to perfection by rapid-fire passing, I found myself with the basketball only four feet from the basket, in the middle of the key. Walton was under the hoop waiting for the shot and rebound. But I saw a ray of light between him and the man he was blocking out, and, ignoring my desire to score, I thought I saw a higher percentage shot. I made a two-foot pass to Walton. He was totally surprised, but caught the pass and scored.

During the post-game team meeting, we all laughed about that play. "*Swen,*" Coach Wooden said with a smile, "*Perhaps you're becoming a bit too unselfish.*"

The remaining character traits that complete the Pyramid of Success seemed to naturally fall into line. Continuing my uphill climb in the area of friendship, loyalty, and cooperation logically resulted because they are the make-up of giving yourself up for the group. Self-control, alertness, initiative, and intentness also improved as my conditioning and skill continued to rise. Poise and confidence were the natural result of all of the foundation blocks below them.

For me personally, the moment that I passed the basketball to Walton is the moment that I had reached the top of the Pyramid. I had the peace of mind Coach Wooden promised I would have if I put in the effort to become the best I could be as a UCLA basketball player.

Conclusion

Guided by his father's words and his own definition of success, and led by his commitment that all students can learn, Coach Wooden preached against comparisons and external rewards, and for focusing on becoming your best. And, although he rarely mentioned the titles of the blocks that formed the Pyramid of Success, he kept our attention on the process, industriousness, enthusiasm, condition, skill, team spirit, and the remaining components of the Pyramid. It was always in the air. In hindsight, it was there in the way he talked to us and most importantly in the example he set for us by the way he lived and taught.

UCLA teams, at the beginning of each season, were bipolar in talent and ability. Yes, the team naturally divided into the aristocracy and a lower class, like the classrooms of my childhood. Comparisons would have continued if

The Great Competitor

Beyond the winning and the goal,
Beyond the glory and the fame,
He finds a flame within his soul,
Born of the spirit of the game.

And where the barriers may wait,
Built up by the opposing gods,
He finds a thrill in bucking fate,
And riding down the endless odds.

Where others wither in the fire,
Or fall below some raw mishap,
Where others lag behind and tire,
And break beneath the handicap,

He finds a new and deeper thrill,
To take him on the uphill spin,
Because the test is greater still,
And something he can revel in.

Grantland Rice

Coach Wooden had allowed intrasquad comparisons and a focus on results, like the score of a game, a league title, or a national championship. But his method of developing individual motivation through his definition of success made it possible for all players, at all levels, to focus on daily improvement. It made it possible even for me—an inexperienced and raw player far behind the rest—to experience success. With Coach Wooden as our teacher, all of us—stars, starters, and reserves—had the same opportunity for success.

I have never forgotten my elementary school days, trying desperately to get that A or B to become an academic star. It never happened. I have also never forgotten my years under the supervision of Coach Wooden, who helped me to adopt a different form of motivation that kept my focus on self-improvement. What he did for me, he also has done for many others. He believes that most students in any classroom will respond to this approach, and there is evidence that he is right.

There are some striking similarities between Coach Wooden's approach and the findings of motivation researchers. From approximately the fourth grade on, students begin to compare their own performance with those of their peers.[11] In many contexts—for example, classrooms and basketball courts—some excel, which is visible to peers. No matter how hard any teacher tries, the students notice that some peers get more external acknowledgments and rewards.

At the same time, grades and test scores begin to loom large. Gradually, students become conditioned to accept others' affirmations or condemnations as a definition of success. If students become totally focused on external signs of success, their motivation and effort can increase or decrease, depending on whether or not those rewards are beyond their reach. Working to gain external signs of success is what researchers call a search for "extrinsic" motivation. The extrinsically motivated student is focused on external rewards—not personal effort and mastery.

In contrast, students who are intrinsically motivated take pleasure in achieving their personal goals. Motivation for them, according to researchers, is not a matter of external rewards but of rewards they generate within themselves.[12] This is why instruction works best if it focuses learners on setting and achieving moderately difficult goals and fosters pride in personal accomplishment. A key element is getting students to focus on personal effort relevant to the goals, and in personal enjoyment of goal-directed activity.[13] For an extensive research program addressed to motivational and emotional factors that is focused on athletes, including those performing at elite levels, see the work by Scanlan and her colleagues.[14]

Look again at what Coach Wooden teaches about motivation—his personal philosophy developed in the 1930s. It is in harmony with behavioral sciences of the 21st century, and a basis for all teachers and coaches who want to motivate their students:

"Success is the peace of mind which is a direct result of the self-satisfaction in knowing that you have made the effort to become the best of which you are capable."

After You Know It All

Beyond the festive caps and gowns,
Beyond the PhDs,
Beyond the books that filled the minds
Of those who earned degrees,

A greater knowledge will commence,
For those who heed the call—
What counts the most is what you learn
After you know it all.

All graduated pedagogues,
When teaching, find in turn,
Those books on what to teach had failed
To show how children learn.

And they will soon discover that
Each child who owns a name,
Is different and unique, and so,
They all don't learn the same.

The classroomed coach who learned, the boys
Are Xs and are Os,
Becomes adept at leadership
The moment that he knows,

Those boys need teacher-shepherds who
Will guide their little lambs
To execute the truths of life
Beyond the diagrams.

Oh decorated graduate,
Once past that college wall,
What counts the most is what you learn,
After you know it all.

Swen Nater

Chapter 3

It's What You Learn After You Know It All That Counts the Most

"I think I learned more my first year of teaching than I ever did of any other year. The second year I think I learned more than any other year following that and the third year, and so on. I think it's the first years where you're definitely going to learn the most. But I hope I learned a little bit each and every year. As I like to say, if I'm through learning, I am through."[1]

Many teachers know exactly what Coach Wooden means by the aphorism borrowed for the title of this chapter. Teachers all over the US and Canada seldom believe their college education and teacher certification, including internships, prepared them for their first teaching job. Some report never learning in college how to teach reading, the depths of simple mathematics, or a child with learning difficulties. Many feel ill-prepared for the challenges of behavior and classroom management, and report they lacked the knowledge and pedagogical skills needed in the early years of their careers. These essentials, they were told in their undergraduate classes, would be acquired through on-the-job learning. Some may be rather disappointed with their alma maters and accuse them of negligence. But before anyone throws stones at college professors, consider other professions.

In general, most college courses do not and were never intended to give graduates specific professional job skills. Accounting, coaching, engineering, computer programming, and many other fields assume that recent graduates are stronger on theory and concept than they are on practice and technique. The fact is, it requires many more than four or five years of university preparation for students to learn everything they need to know to be an accomplished professional in any field. Indeed, one of the defining qualities of a *profession* is that its practitioners are life-long learners who never stop learning new knowledge and skills.

For teachers, life-long learning is a necessity if they are to keep up with changing curricula, technology, and students. New and more demanding subject matter standards have been adopted by many school districts over the past two decades, partly in response to global challenges and partly in reaction to public expectations that education will prepare young people for high tech jobs. The student population always changes as well, both in experiences, expectations, and background. Those born into the multi-media, computer age are very different from the youth of the middle third of the 20th century. The increasing diversity of the U.S. population is another change for which teachers have to learn new and different approaches in which to best relate to their students.

Courtesy of Indiana State University
By the time he accepted his first collegiate coaching job at Indiana State University in 1946, Coach Wooden had already begun researching the intricacies of the game of basketball.

On the first day of eighth grade in the 1960s, I recall my math teacher saying something that scared me to death: "The New Math." Multiplied tingles still go up and down my spine when I hear that phrase. When he said, "The New Math," the expression on his face was telling. As the days went by, it became obvious—The New Math was not something of which he was fond. The school district had adopted it as a new curriculum, and it was a drastic change from the old one, both in content and instructional strategy. My teacher was required to understand it and know how to teach it after just a few days of workshops conducted just prior to the start of the school year. Although he was interested in new ways of teaching, the changeover to a totally new approach was a major challenge, and a lot of the learning required had to be done on teachers' own time. When I became a teacher myself, I was better able to understand. With the increasing pressures to raise standards and achievement, in the 21st century more than ever teachers have to be life-long learners in order to keep up with the times.

Coach Wooden anticipated, by decades, the need for teachers to actively pursue individual intellectual and professional development after they leave college. In fact, he went one idea better and got an extraordinarily early start on a lifetime commitment to continuous improvement. While still a student-athlete at Purdue University, he interviewed opposing coaches and players to add to his knowledge of basketball and coaching. Already committed to a career as a teacher and coach, he began keeping notes on the strategies and tactics used by opposing teams and their coaches. Even after a fiercely fought game—win or lose—he would approach the opposing coach to get the details on something that had worked well that day (e.g., a particular method of team rebounding). Unfortunately, somehow the notes went missing before he left Purdue, a loss he still regrets more than 70 years later.

Throughout his career, he practiced continuous improvement through steady research. He continued this practice when he became a teacher and coach, and he continued doing it even as national championship banners were hung one after another in the rafters of UCLA's Pauley Pavilion. Even the year before he retired, he searched for ways to improve his teaching and his program.

"I learned more in my early years, of course, but you can always learn. It's what you learn after you know it all that matters most."[2]

Coach Wooden believes continuous improvement is essential to everyone—players and coaches, students and teachers.

"We must get our players to believe that the best way to improve the team is to improve themselves, and, in doing so, we must not lose sight of the fact that the same principle holds true in regard to the coach."[3]

How he went about improving his own teaching is worth a chapter in its own right, for it was fundamental to his success as a teacher. It's a method that every teacher at every level of education can successfully use.

John Wooden's Method of Continuous Improvement Through Research

Research of any kind is best designed by first clarifying the purpose. The purpose of teacher research is for the benefit of the students.

"The purpose of self-improvement is, of course, to help students improve. He [the coach] must continually be exploring for ways to improve himself in order that he may improve others and welcome every person and everything that can be helpful to him. A wise motto might be, 'Others, too, have brains.'"[4]

Immediately after accepting the head coaching position at UCLA in 1948, Coach Wooden began to employ an organized research and development system, which allowed him to make substantial improvements each year in how he taught basketball. At the conclusion of each basketball season, during the off-season his self-improvement research began. He chose only one topic for each off-season study (e.g., defensive rebounding, free-throw shooting, etc.).The goal was to uncover all he could learn about a specific subject, draw conclusions, and apply it to his teaching.

Coach Wooden's premise was the assumption that all the essential truths about each topic existed "somewhere," but scattered across many sources. Some of those truths were in books, some in the thoughts of successful coaches and athletes, and others were, perhaps, in places he never considered. Some ideas were his own (e.g., many of his ideas on free-throw shooting—as a player he once made more than 130 in succession), but needed testing, refinement, and elaboration, just as any researcher tests the theories that guide investigations. Thus, Coach's approach was essentially similar to empirical investigations in all fields of inquiry. What follows is the story of one off-season study he conducted in which the focus was free-throw shooting. This story is used to describe and illustrate each of the sequence of steps he used to conduct his investigations.

Defining a Research Question

Coach Wooden's first step in the sequence was the development of a clear idea of what he wanted to investigate. Although he focused on a topic or question, he also kept an open mind so that he might also notice the unexpected.

"There are many possible questions and topics to consider, but it's important to choose the right one. When making my choice, I kept the following things in mind. Was it a team weakness last season? Will I need it next year? Is it too broad of a subject? Is it related to another subject previously studied or not yet studied? If the subject is related to a subject not yet studied, I planned on taking the latter on the next off-season. That seemed natural to me.

"I also believe in predetermining what it is you are looking for. For example, when studying free-throw shooting, one of the things I wanted to find out was the percentage of practice time successful coaches provided for the practice of it. I also was interested in finding if there was a better way to make free-throw shooting practice more game-like. During games, free throws come sporadically and unexpectedly. Most coaches, during practice sessions, donate a certain amount of time for just shooting free throws. I was not satisfied with that approach because it did not simulate game conditions. So, I started my study with those questions in mind. Of course, I remained open-minded so that I could learn other things that may come up, and often times, they did."[5]

The year Coach Wooden researched free-throw shooting was typical. He began by asking the questions, "What do coaches do to make their teams become high-percentage free-throw shooting teams? What do the successful coaches have in common?"

Before collecting new data, Coach read every book he could find on the subject of free throws, making and filing copious notes. In addition to books, other resources were searched, such as *Scholastic Coach* and *The Athletic Journal*, two publications that contained articles written by successful coaches. From library research and what his own experience taught him, he assembled

Courtesy of UCLA Photography

Each off-season, Coach Wooden chose a specific aspect of the game of basketball to study, reading every book possible about each particular subject.

substantial data, but not enough to answer all of his questions. Usually it is only successful and highly visible coaches that publish books and articles, but Coach Wooden knew there were other coaches who did not write books but had developed excellent free-throw shooting teams. To learn what they did, he would have to do an empirical study.

Selecting a Sample

He began his study by reviewing free-throw statistics on college teams around the nation. In the 1940s and 1950s, statistics on every team in the country were not nearly as easy to locate as today. By paying close attention to the teams who competed against him, and recalling some excellent coaches he had met or heard about in the past (books, hearsay, coaches' clinics, etc.), he identified six teams with free-throw shooting percentages in the mid to high seventieth percentile. Back then, just as today, any team that averaged better than 70% for the season was considered a very good free-throw shooting squad. Coach Wooden was curious to know how and why those teams demonstrated excellence.

Courtesy of Tom Campbell/Gold & Black Illustrated

Coach Wooden's principles have been adopted by countless modern-day coaches, including Gene Keady, who is
the all-time winningest coach at Purdue University,
Coach Wooden's alma mater.

Developing a Survey Instrument

To make his investigation systematic, he designed a survey instrument that
included the questions which his experience and library research had identified as crucial to a full understanding of free-throw shooting. All the questions
were open-ended, meaning that his respondents could answer as they pleased,
rather than being forced to choose among pre-selected answers. It's a familiar
distinction to any student: an essay vs. a multiple-choice exam, except in this
case the respondents just report rather than write their responses.

The open-ended instrument thus required the participating coaches to
explain in their own words how they taught free-throw shooting. Some of
his questions, for example, were, "*What particular routine do you teach your
players? How much practice time do you set aside for free-throw shooting? To
what do you attribute your team's success? Please list, and explain, what you
believe to be the fundamentals of free-throw shooting.*" Room was provided for

as much information as a coach wanted to add, and the participating coach would be encouraged to bring up topics and issues not covered in the original instrument.

Procedures

Next, Coach Wooden telephoned each selected coach, explaining his project and asking if he would be so kind as to participate by filling out a survey of questions, all relating to free-throw shooting. He stressed that he was looking for brief, but clear information, rather than answers that were more time consuming. His surveys were usually sent out two weeks after the last game of the season, and he asked if the participating coach would return it by no later than October 1. Practice for the next season always started on October 15, and he needed time to organize the data, analyze it, and implement findings into his practice plans. Most coaches that he invited to participate eagerly accepted. Coach also offered to send his final results to the participants, if they were interested.

Interviews were also conducted with exceptional free-throw shooters. Living in Los Angeles, Coach Wooden had access to many professional basketball players who were usually very willing to answer questions. One player he interviewed was one of the greatest free-throw shooters of all time, Bill Sharman. From his colleagues, Coach Wooden learned how to develop a good free-throw shooting team, but from individuals, such as Sharman, he learned about technique. He was particularly interested in the position of the feet. Was the right foot placed slightly ahead of the left? How far apart were Sharman's feet when he shot free throws? Another area of interest was the position of the elbow, from the start of the shot to the finish. Coach learned a lot from Sharman and several other professional and former professional players. In addition, he already had notes on his own players. Every time he learned something, he filed it away.

Data Collection

Books, articles, surveys, and players all provided a plethora of valuable information. Coach Wooden was careful not to analyze the data or jump to any conclusions until all of the information was collected. He created files for each coach he surveyed and/or read, complete with name, school, address, phone number, and any other information he may have gathered before and during the research. He also telephoned each coach who returned a survey.

"When I received a survey, I immediately telephoned the coach who sent it to me and thanked him. It was the right thing to do, of course."[6]

Data Analysis

When all data was collected, Coach began analyzing it. This is where he was at his best.

"I have always considered myself average in many areas. However, my strength is in analyzing players and statistics. I loved digging deep into information to see what I could find. As I began going through each coach's folder, I looked for things they all had in common. For example, every coach and player made mention of the importance of the elbow position. However, most only covered the elbow on the release of the basketball, when the elbow was already above the head. But a couple of them stressed the importance of starting the elbow in the proper position, above the knee. Others thought the position of the feet were important. Bill Sharman was one of those. When several coaches and players stressed the same fundamental or strategy, I took note and considered it to be of significance."[7]

When analyzing data, researchers often encounter "exceptions to the rule," what they sometimes call anomalies or outliers. Outliers are findings that don't seem to fit. If the researcher fails to notice these exceptions they may not only end up with distorted statistics, they might fail to discover something new and interesting to pursue. Like any curious researcher, Coach Wooden was also alert to the possibilities that outliers offer, and he provided the following amusing example, which nonetheless yielded an important and unexpected discovery.

"During the free-throw study, as was true for some of my other topics, I found one person who was successful in this area, but went about things in an unusual manner. In other words, his teams, year after year, had unusually good free-throw percentages. I found no other coach who did it his way.

"Apparently, he believed free-throw shooting was so important he devoted about half of each practice session to it and also required his players to shoot between practices and the entire off-season. Since the objective of my study was to improve my team's free-throw percentage and give us another edge to win, I was curious as to how this coach's teams fared in the win-loss columns. To my surprise, his teams were unsuccessful in this department, even though his talent was comparable to that of his opponents. They didn't win many games, but oh my, they could really shoot free throws. My conclusion was, the more time a team spends on free-throw shooting, the better it becomes, but I also realized there would be a point of diminishing returns.

"This immediately led me to analyze the rest of the data. I was curious to know where that point of diminishing returns was. In other words, I wanted to know how much was too much and exactly how much practice time was needed."[8]

Studying this unusual case led Coach deeper into his study. For the coach who focused so much on free-throw practice, the free-throw drills were always separate parts of the practice. In other words, time was set aside for the team to do nothing else but shoot free throws. The question was, is this the right method, or should free-throw shooting be integrated into practice?

"I was curious to see if other coaches used the same method. Logically, I thought, since, during basketball games, free-throw shooting was sporadic, the same should be done during the practice session. After all, practice is preparation for games. The most free throws any player would shoot in a row, during games, is two. Therefore, the same should hold true in practice. As logical as that seemed to me, when analyzing the information I received from the other sources, I saw the field divided in this area.

"I called some coaches to find out their reasons for both methods. What I discovered was, the teachers who separated free-throw shooting into drills used that method because that's the way they were taught. The ones who integrated free throws into the practice session did so for the same reasons I had— it's more game-like.

"For free throws, I found that the vast majority of basketball teachers did not follow the concept that 'practice is preparation for games.' I made a note to work out a method of making free-throw shooting during practices a more game-like experience."[9]

Some outliers, at first, may seem so odd that it's tempting to dismiss them (e.g., the coach who spent half of practice time on free-throw shooting). However, this outlier helped to confirm two important principles: First, the more time on task, the better the results. Second, by incorporating free-throw drills into practice it was possible to give players more game-like experiences.

"During scrimmages, which were a significant part of our practice sessions, when one player would replace another in the scrimmage, the one who went out was required to make a predetermined amount of free throws in a row before he was allowed to substitute for another player. As a result, the players were practicing free throws after participating in strenuous drills, which made the free-throw shooting more similar to game conditions. I believe because of this new way of teaching free throws, we increased our team percentage during games."[10]

Drawing Conclusions

After all of the data was collected and analyzed, Coach Wooden developed his data-based conclusions. The conclusions for his free-throw study are presented in Table 3.1.

Table 3.1: Summary of Free-Throw Shooting Study Results

INDIVIDUAL FUNDAMENTALS

1. Style, such as where to stand, routine, and elbow position are taught, if the player is not a good shooter. If he is already a good free-throw shooter, don't tamper with success.
2. For those who need help:
   a. Feet a little wider than the shoulders.
   b. Balance.
   c. Right-handers shoot slightly to the left of center and left-handers shoot slightly to the right.
   d. Shoulders should be squared to the backboard.
   e. Elbow should start above the knee, never stop moving, and end up above the ear on the follow through.
   f. Arc should be medium, not too high and not too low.
   g. Player should follow through as if he has an extended arm that can reach into the basket. However, balance must be maintained.
   h. Player should keep his eye on the front of the rim.
   i. Head should follow the shot but no leaning.
   j. Player should take three dribbles, look up at the basket and shoot. No staring at the basket too long, or shooting too quickly.
   k. After follow through, the arm should retreat in the same path as when the shot was executed.

TEAM FUNDAMENTALS

1. Free-throw shooting should be integrated into the practice session and should be as game-like as possible.
2. We must place pressure on the player when he shoots free throws in practice.
3. We must have players shoot free throws when they are in various states of physical and mental fatigue.
4. A significant number of free throws must be taken toward the end of the practice session, in game-like conditions.

Conclusion

Coach Wooden is the first to say that the conditions under which he worked at UCLA were very different from the everyday circumstances of most teachers. As one teacher noted, "I don't have a lot of Kareem Abdul-Jabbar and Bill Walton all-star scholars in my classroom." Neither can most teachers be so focused on a single subject, or enjoy the support that comes with being the head coach at a Division I university. But that does not mean the basic principles of Coach Wooden's continuous improvement strategy cannot work. In fact, there's growing evidence that it can, and that done properly teachers find it useful and effective.[11]

Teachers are asking for and getting new kinds of professional development opportunities that bear some remarkable similarities to Coach Wooden's personal system for continuous development. Indeed, the National Staff Development Council has adopted standards for high quality teacher development, and one of the first on their list is this: High quality programs require and foster a norm of *continuous teaching improvement*.

So, how can teachers begin to use ideas based on Coach Wooden's continuous improvement approach? One place to start is finding like-minded colleagues to form a team willing to work on improving classroom teaching and student learning. The key to success is a laser-focus on improving student learning.[12] Teachers who collaborate to improve their teaching (and their students' learning) don't get hung up on philosophical debates about things they can't change. They follow one of Coach's favorite maxims: *"Do not permit what you cannot do to interfere with what you can do."*[13] One thing any teacher can do is look at his or her own practices and search for ways that will help students learn more, just as Coach did for five decades—right up to his last year when his final team won a 10th national title for UCLA.

The next step is to identify the critical things students need to learn during the course of an academic year (e.g., how to write an essay, comprehend complex readings, or understand place value in mathematics). Once focused on a collaborative goal for improving teaching and learning, teachers can begin the steady work of examining and improving their own practice. An important part of this step is joint analysis of student work that can yield powerful ideas for improving teaching.[14]

One reason for optimism that this is a practical approach is a nation-wide system used in Japan called "lesson study."[15] Like the approach Coach Wooden used, the goal of lesson study is gradual, incremental improvements in teaching over time. As one book on the subject noted,

"Japan has given teachers themselves primary responsibility for improving the classroom practice ... [through] the continuous process of school-based professional development that Japanese teachers engage in once they begin their teaching careers.... Participation in school-based professional development groups is considered part of the teacher's job in Japan."[16]

None of these ideas, including Coach Wooden's, are going to lead to "quick fixes." There are many wonderful things about American society, but the addiction to quick fixes for complicated problems is not one of them. Nowhere is this addiction more evident than in the willingness to believe that solving major problems in our schools is just around the corner, that some new fad will do the trick.

No, it won't, no more than "tricks of the trade" can be substituted for "learning the trade," as Coach often says. Like so many other challenges and dilemmas, he has a solution for how to improve teaching that is all at once powerful, simple, and hard to argue with.

"When you improve a little each day, eventually big things occur.... Not tomorrow, not the next day, but eventually a big gain is made. Don't look for the big, quick improvement. Seek the small improvement one day at a time. That's the only way it happens—and when it happens, it lasts."[17]

"Perhaps the gravest failing of our current system of teacher preparation and certification is the many teachers who lack deep knowledge of the subjects that they teach. While most public school teachers are certified by their states, extensive college-level study in the teaching field is not always a prerequisite for certification. Moreover, teachers are often assigned to courses outside their main teaching field as a cost-saving measure or administrative convenience, because of shortages in advanced subjects like math and science, or because of high teacher turnover in particular schools."

National Council of Teacher Quality[1]

Chapter 4

You Can't Teach What You Don't Possess

Most of us can remember at least one teacher whose passion for a particular subject was contagious. For example, a coworker of mine at Costco told me about a fifth-grade teacher at her daughter's school who loved studying and talking about the oceans. Lisa, my co-worker's daughter, caught the fever and, as a result, read nearly every available book on the subjects all through elementary, middle, and high school. She then went on to earn degrees in oceanography, marine biology, and biology.

But Lisa would not have become interested nor become a sponge for knowledge had her teacher not coupled her enthusiasm with a deep knowledge about oceans. The prerequisite of passion is deep subject matter knowledge. It's not clear whether the passion preceded the deep understanding or vice versa, but both were present and instrumental in rousing Lisa's interest in learning more.

Student interest is directly proportional to the depth and breadth of teachers' knowledge; and student interest is vital to effective teaching.

John Wooden's Knowledge of Basketball

A clue to the depth of Coach Wooden's knowledge of basketball is the size and breadth of his textbook titled *Practical Modern Basketball*.[2] Building on the "basketball curriculum" he had begun writing in the 1930s, the third edition is 452 pages long, with 77 and 63 pages devoted to team offense and defensive strategies, respectively. Other sections address coaching philosophy and general concerns (77 pp.), individual offense (69 pp.), obtaining possession of the ball (13

Coach Wooden did a masterful job of passing along his knowledge of the nuances of the game of basketball to his players.

pp.), and miscellaneous drills (97 pp.). Unlike many curricula, this one was written by the teacher himself, and includes his own experiences and research (Chapter 2), including all he learned from his own coaches when he was playing, and later on from many coaching peers and his own assistants. Other coaches have written books on basketball, but the sheer volume of information in Coach Wooden's text has seldom been matched.

For example, the section on team offense contains many diagrams, complete with explanations, detailing the high-post offense system (which he used almost exclusively through his career) and its every possible option. The offensive system is so complete that there is an option to answer virtually every possible defensive countermove an opponent may employ. In addition, special plays and out-of-bounds plays are also described and explained in detail.

Although such detailed analysis of basketball plays is common among coaches, my experience as a professional player and college coach confirmed for me that it was Coach Wooden's extensive details and the many nuances he added to his basketball curriculum that made the difference between UCLA teams simply being good and winning championships.

For example, I have rarely seen any coach, past or present, college or pro, exhibit such a comprehensive grasp of the benefits rebounding and defensive balance can provide a team. Specifically, Coach Wooden's offense was designed to be balanced (ball side, or "strong side," and the side away from the ball, or "weak side") at all times, especially when a shot was taken. Balance allowed each of his players to move quickly to their designated rebounding and defensive balance positions. The three players close to the basket created a rebounding triangle, surrounding the basket. The player taking the shot (the "long rebounder") moved to the area just below the free-throw line, and the player on the weak-side perimeter (called the "protector") moved towards the half-court line. The shooter, who moved to the area just below the free-throw line, was responsible for rebounds that bounced out beyond the three inside rebounders. The protector was responsible for protecting the far basket should the opponents gain possession and begin a fast break. This post-shot alignment occurred after every shot with absolutely no exceptions, and any player who neglected to do so was essentially sending a message to Coach that he didn't want to play.

Coach Wooden considered the following details critical because they resulted in three ingredients, all essential to winning basketball:

1. Extra rebounding opportunities—An offensive rebound equals an opponent turnover, or loss of possession. The team with the most possessions has a distinct advantage for scoring the most points in a game.

2. Eliminate opponent fast breaks—With two guards back to stop the advancement of the ball, should the opponents obtain the rebound, the three inside rebounders were able to sprint to the opposite end of the court, completing a sound team defensive alignment.

3. 2-2-1 full-court press preparation—Players in prime position to set up the 2-2-1 full-court press, should the shot go in.

One result of Coach Wooden's deep knowledge of basketball was fast-paced, exciting practices that were economical, allowing a maximum amount of instruction to be packed into a two-hour practice session. The nature of these practices, and the role that Coach's knowledge played, was revealed by a study of his teaching.[3] Initially, the researchers paid little attention to the subject matter he was teaching.[4] Like most teaching researchers of that era, they were focused on pedagogical techniques, and were curious to know if and how a celebrated coach like Coach Wooden used them. It was a great opportunity to answer a basic theoretical question—what teaching techniques are used by a teacher with an objective record of success who has students of exceptional talent and motivation?

Although the researchers were examining how frequently Coach used positive reinforcement, or modeled a correct action, etc., unanticipated features of his teaching were impossible to ignore. The researchers were impressed by his tightly organized practices, run with clock-like precision. Players moved from drill to drill quickly and efficiently, and the intensity level was kept at a remarkably high level.

"We were startled to discover that the educational psychology techniques we expected to see were seldom used. Yes, Coach Wooden used positive reinforcement and modeling (two favorites of educational psychology at the time), but mostly what he did was deliver information about how to play basketball. He packed into every practice and every sentence an enormous amount of information. Wooden was teaching a rich basketball curriculum and delivered information at precisely the moments it would help his students learn the most."[5]

The rapid-fire, frequent corrections during practices (described in Chapter 1) were partly a product of his planning (see Chapter 5), but they also were based on his deep, analytic knowledge of the sport. He could spot even the tiniest imperfection and provide a coherent explanation and rationale for why there was a better way. His knowledge was also revealed during the half-hour individual sessions conducted before regular practices began. Anytime one of his players asked a question, Coach had an immediate, comprehensible answer or provided a demonstration of a specific action. The ability to discriminate and explain alternatives, just as in the classroom, depends on subject matter knowledge.

It is an amazing experience for me to sit with Coach while he watches and comments on a video of a practice. Even at the age of 94, there is no limit to the knowledge and ideas he commands. I've seen him spot a seemingly minor miscue on the videotape and explain two, three, or four problems that the error could cause. He will stand and demonstrate alternatives, and explain in detail the advantages and disadvantages of each, what a player should watch for, and the options that are available at each point in a play. Just when I think I've learned everything I could about a given offensive play, he comes up with another nuance or option I never saw or learned even after a decade of playing professional basketball.

But Coach not only mastered offenses and defenses, he also constantly worked to deepen his knowledge of other areas that he believed were essential—conditioning, skill, and team spirit. Although all coaches strive for their players to be conditioned, skilled, and team oriented, there is much more to these than the casual observer might imagine.

Each year, Coach Wooden's team was considered to be the best conditioned in the nation, more fundamentally sound than any other, and exhibiting superior teamwork. Sports columns of the day wrote of the "9:00 lightning," which described a common event in UCLA games. Typically, at some point late in the first half, the UCLA full-court press and superior stamina would begin to wear down the visiting team and the players would struggle to get the ball past the half-court line. The Bruins would steal the ball again and again, causing the opposing point guard to look toward his coach with a frustrated and puzzled expression. Even if UCLA missed a shot, it would grab more than its fair share of offensive rebounds. Combined with the turnovers created by its full-court press, it allowed UCLA to start a run of unanswered baskets and build an insurmountable lead. In some years, UCLA won games by an average of 30 points, and few outcomes were in doubt past halftime. One of the reasons for the overwhelming victories was Coach Wooden's deep knowledge about conditioning, skill, and team spirit.

Conditioning

Ask any coach what "conditioning" means, and most will say something about physical conditioning. But for Coach Wooden, good physical conditioning was dependent on moral and mental conditioning. To be in top physical condition (the ability to play an entire basketball game without physical fatigue hindering performance) players must be able to generate 100% physical effort in practice. But they cannot possibly give their all in practice if they stayed out late the night before, or if they consumed substances detrimental to allowing them to be at their best the following day. For that reason, physical conditioning was contingent upon moral conditioning. Coach preached about and insisted on his players taking care of themselves outside of practice by often repeating, "*What you do between practices can do more harm for your conditioning than practice can help you.*"[6]

Another hindrance to performance is frustration and lack of concentration. Players who were easily distracted by the crowd and its noise, opponents, or officials were not mentally conditioned. To Coach Wooden, mental conditioning included emotional conditioning. He taught us how to handle emotional highs and lows. He often said, "*For every high, there's a low. I don't want you to get too excited about a game and get pumped up so high that, should things not happen as they should, your emotions will drop.*"[7]

Most of us are familiar with the pre-game speeches of Knute Rockne, the legendary former Notre Dame football coach, who motivated his teams with "Win one for the Gipper" speeches before they sprinted onto the football field to face their foes. In contrast, Coach Wooden's pre-game talks were short, to the point, and not in the least melodramatic. He wanted his players to remain emotionally balanced heading into a contest.

Instead of emotionally armoring his teams to do battle, he stressed doing your best so that whatever the outcome, you could walk off the court at the end of the game holding your head up knowing you put forth your best effort (see Chapter 2). Coaches who practice charging up their teams emotionally may not understand Coach Wooden's reasoning, but they cannot argue with his success. According to him, teaching sound emotional conditioning is one of those "little things" that may mean the difference between failure and success.

He believes the concept of multi-dimensional conditioning (physical, mental, and emotional) is transferable to the classroom. In fact, when teaching high school English, he conditioned his students.

"Certainly moral, mental, emotional, and physical condition is part of being a good classroom student, although, in the classroom, the physical takes a back seat to the other three. We can, and should, teach all students to have integrity, in school and out of school. This will lead to a better ability to think deeply for an entire school day. And, I made a conscious effort to train my students to keep under emotional control. I believe all of this helped them in their education."[8]

Skill

"The close games are usually lost, rather than won. What I mean by that is, games are mostly won because of the opponent making mistakes during crucial moments."[9] Most coaches would agree with this statement, but what do the coaches do about it? Coach Wooden conducted detailed studies of the types of end-of-game errors that determine outcomes. He concluded that most mistakes were caused by weaknesses in the basic fundamentals of basketball skills (e.g., simple dribbling errors, passing into an interception, catching the ball off balance resulting in an illegal extra step, etc.).

For that reason, while most other teams were weaned from the basic fundamental drills, Coach Wooden had his UCLA basketball players spend a liberal amount of time each practice from October to April on the building blocks of basketball. Those who observed practice sessions—who were few because they were closed to the public—were stunned to see the top team in the country devoting a significant percentage of practice time on simple pivots, imaginary jump shots, cross-over dribbles, change-of-pace/change-of-direction cutting, and shadow rebounding, performing most of the drills without the use of a basketball. Most teams practice fundamental skills during the early portion of the season, but Coach's practice plans at the end of the season included the same drills as the ones he used at the beginning of the season. The last practice of the season, the day before the NCAA championship game, observers were shocked to see us meticulously perfect the basic building blocks of the game, while the other team spent their time running plays designed to score against our defense and practice defensive stunts they needed to utilize against our offense. Some may have questioned whether fundamentals were overemphasized during Coach Wooden's practices, but the answer is in his record.

His basketball curriculum featured perfection of the basic skills because he believed that one mistake committed in the NCAA championship game could result in defeat. As a result, his UCLA teams won 10 national championships,

Courtesy of UCLA Photography
Basic fundamental drills were performed every practice throughout each season by Coach Wooden's teams.

partly because the opponents committed pivotal errors in the final minutes of the game.

The effectiveness of giving basic skill work consistent priority is not limited to basketball or other sports. Coach Wooden believes it is, and should be, applicable to the classroom as well. "*There are fundamentals to reading, spelling, writing, mathematics, and most every school subject. For English, the teacher should not assume the students are accomplished in the fundamentals such as proper spelling technique, sentence structure, and reading. Although it may seem mundane and routine, regular practice in the basics strengthens the students' foundations in those areas.*"[10]

But stressing fundamentals is not enough. Coach teaches that the purpose of being fundamentally sound is to provide *a foundation on which individual creativity and imagination can flourish.*[11] It is a false dichotomy, he insists, to claim that one must either focus on fundamental skills or on higher-order learning and understanding. One rests on the other, and both should be properly taught concurrently from the onset (see Chapter 6 for more on skill vs. understanding issue).

Team Spirit

Nowhere does Coach Wooden's deep knowledge manifest itself better than in his unique view of team play—in particular, which players he selected to be the "regulars" who received the majority of the playing time. UCLA teams were divided into two groups, the regulars and those who practiced but didn't see much game time. Usually, there were only seven "regular" players.

Because he had a recruiting advantage—due in part to his teams' successes, the UCLA academic opportunities, the surroundings, and Coach Wooden himself—his teams were normally 12-players deep. All 12 were physically talented and capable of being starters at many other programs. But Coach did not choose his regulars based on physical talent or ability alone; he had a very different approach. It had everything to do with "teamwork."

His approach departs from the norm because most coaches typically play the most physically talented players. Those who can run fast, jump high, or shoot well are going to be regulars and the offensive/defensive system is devised accordingly. In that approach, roles on a team are designed around the "stars," or most physically talented players. But Coach Wooden had a system with predetermined roles, into which players had to fit if they wanted to be regulars. Each position on the floor—guards, forwards, and center—had a specific job description. When all players performed their jobs well, the team succeeded. If any one did not, the team was not achieving its potential.

Here is the interesting and strange part—failing to fulfill a role is not limited to a lack of ability to perform. Failure can also come from a physically gifted player who tries to do more than his role requires. In the early 1970s, one very talented player had a difficult time understanding this concept and it kept him relegated to the bench. That player, however, eventually learned to buy into Coach's approach.

Sidney Wicks, fresh out of Santa Monica Community College, joined an already great UCLA team that included such stars as Mike Warren, Lucius Allen, and Lewis Alcindor (Kareem Abdul-Jabaar). Another player, Lynn Shackleford, who played the wing on Lewis' side, was limited in what he could do, but perfectly performed his assigned team role. Although Wicks was probably one of the most talented individual players in the nation, he sat on the bench while Shackleford played instead.

One afternoon, Wicks approached Coach Wooden privately to make the case that he was more talented than Shackleford and should be the regular. But Coach's answer was a revelation for Wicks and speaks volumes. He said, *"Yes, Sidney. I agree with you. And it's a shame you're letting Lynn beat you out."*

After understanding the player fits the role, not vice versa, and that there was no place for individual glory through flashy play that compromised Coach Wooden's team approach, Wicks developed into one of the greatest players in college basketball history. This happened because Wicks learned a portion of Coach's deep understanding of team spirit and the roles each regular player must fulfill. Just knowing some sound pedagogy can benefit a teacher, but without deeply understanding the system of knowledge being taught, a teacher cannot see the big picture. And, without the big picture, the components, like "the player fits the role," don't make sense.

Conclusion

Given the number of U.S. instructors teaching out of their field of study, the standard set by Coach Wooden is a formidable one. He believes, and the research confirms, that you cannot teach well what you do not know very well. There are at least two kinds of knowledge this includes. The first is the conventional definition of knowledge: you know how to play basketball, or do algebra. You took the classes, and passed the courses. The second is the kind of knowledge that is essential to teaching: pedagogical content knowledge which is having the ability to *make content comprehensible to learners*. This includes

"The most regularly taught topics in one's subject area, the most useful forms of representation of those ideas, the most powerful analogies, illustrations, examples, explanations, demonstrations—in a word, the ways of representing and formulating the subject that make it comprehensible to others. Since there are no single most powerful forms of representation, the teacher must have at hand a veritable armamentarium of alternative forms of representation, some of which derive from research whereas others originate in the wisdom of practice."[12]

A young teacher might learn a great deal of subject matter in a college major. In his or her teacher education courses, he or she might also learn some of what it takes to make subjects comprehensible to be learners. But few seriously believe that those entering the profession from college know all the pedagogical content knowledge (PCK) they'll need. Realistically, when they leave pre-service programs they'll need to know how to learn PCK on the job.[13]

Unfortunately, American schools are not generally organized as places of learning for teachers, and for the development of pedagogical content knowledge in particular. "The assumption that teachers can create and maintain those conditions which make school learning and school living stimulating for children, without those same conditions existing for teachers, has no warrant in the history of man."[14]

How did Coach Wooden come to possess deep subject matter knowledge? He took it upon himself to create his own research and development system (see Chapter 3). Teachers can, too, and many do in fact pursue their own self-improvement studies. But think how much more teachers might learn and improve if schools provided the materials and means for them to deepen their

Courtesy of Brent Clayton/Duke University Photography

Duke University coach Mike Krzyzewski was the recipient of the 2000 Legends of Coaching Award, which recognizes coaches who exemplify Coach Wooden's high standards of coaching success and personal achievement.

knowledge in collaboration with their colleagues—the ones who are teaching the same subjects and topics. Happily, there are some indications that school districts around the nation are beginning to realize the importance of continuous teacher learning of pedagogical content knowledge and instructional alternatives, and teachers are asking for school-site learning opportunities directly related to what they are responsible to teach.[15]

In addition to supporting teachers' continuous development of pedagogical content knowledge, there is a related problem that remains unsolved. A long time ago, John Dewey, an influential thinker on education in the twentieth century, said that the saddest thing about American schools is that when good teachers retire all their professional knowledge goes with them. There is now in America no way to accumulate teachers' professional and pedagogical content knowledge, store it, validate it, and share it. If teachers are lucky enough to teach with colleagues of great knowledge, they might have an opportunity to observe or talk to them. But it's a haphazard system at best.

Just before he retired from the Senate, John Glenn chaired a commission on the improvement of teaching. One of its recommendations was the development of national, regional, and local multi-media knowledge bases. Because it is now possible to store video and related data that can be accessed over the Internet, teachers could have immediate access to the best ideas accompanied by vivid examples of alternative practices. Done properly, these knowledge bases will have been sifted, evaluated, and verified, yielding standard practices that distinguish a true profession.[16]

Digital libraries are likely to have more impact if they are built around vivid images of practice and not words. Teaching is complex and hard to capture in words. Words mean different things to different people, so too much energy in education goes to debating the merits of different practices. The TIMSS Video Study confirmed what many already knew—the words used to talk about teaching often reference quite different things, so that what one means by problem-solving, for example, is markedly different from what another means.[17] In one laboratory, there has been some promising results using video lesson cases for teachers to study and learn from (for an example, see http://www.lessonlab.com).

It's too soon to know if these efforts will make a difference. But the answer to the following question will surely underscore the promise of the concept. Would it be of use to teachers and coaches if they could watch fully documented examples of Coach Wooden at work, complete with his comments time-linked to the videos? Would it be helpful to study his lesson plans and then study a video to see how he implemented them on the practice floor? Would it stimulate discussion among teachers if these and other lesson cases were available on the Internet, and could be examined by individual or collaborating teams?

Sadly, there are no known films or videos of Coach teaching on the practice court. Although his book *Practical Modern Basketball* provides rich information on all his knowledge, there are no visual records from which the rest of us could learn. Just like every great teacher who leaves the profession, we are in danger of losing the knowledge Coach Wooden accumulated and tested over a lifetime of teaching.

Failing To Prepare

If you founded your house on the movable sand,
And have failed to secure a firm hold on the land,
Take advice from the Lord and His Biblical tale,
If you fail to prepare, you're preparing to fail.

If you squander your time on the tricks of the trade,
On discovering just how a shortcut is made,
You've neglected the work and your skills are but frail.
If you fail to prepare, you're preparing to fail.

Can you fathom a sailboat alone on the sea,
And the storm and the waves dancing violently?
Like a crew that's untrained for the tempest and gale,
If you fail to prepare, you're preparing to fail.

If a cross-country runner trains only a stint,
And he practices simply by running a sprint,
He will make it part way down the arduous trail.
If you fail to prepare, you're preparing to fail.

Any seeds that are sown will not vanish or spoil,
If they're spread on the tilled and the fertilized soil.
It's a soil that's prepared for the seeds in the pail.
If you fail to prepare, you're preparing to fail.

If you want no excuses, no worries or frets,
If you want peace of mind, ever void of regrets,
Let the wisdom sequester you far from the wail.
If you fail to prepare, you're preparing to fail.

Swen Nater

Chapter 5

Failure to Prepare is Preparing to Fail

Teachers can usually recall a lesson that dissolved into confusion, bordering on or becoming chaos. It might have been their first days and weeks on the job. It might have been a time they tried to teach a lesson while being sorely unprepared. Sooner or later, every teacher learns how indispensable planning is to student learning—and personal survival. Those early days of trial and error may eventually make for humorous "war stories" to share with friends. But at the time there was little to laugh about, and a lot to yearn for. I had one of those painful but instructive experiences.

A Painful Lesson

After I retired from professional basketball, I became a college teacher and basketball coach. Whether teaching mathematics or basketball, like everyone else I learned that failing to plan was planning to fail. A vivid lesson came at the beginning of my second year teaching basketball. Still new to the profession, I learned that year that I had a lot to learn about teaching and planning.

After a far-from-great first year, I knew I needed a plan that would keep me on track the entire season. The first day of practice was only two weeks away when I finally started to formulate a plan. I didn't know where to begin. Should I start diving into books for suggestions? Should I try to recall what we had done last year? The pencil remained on the desk. If I could find last year's lesson plans, will they provide any information to help me improve? And what was that one out-of-bounds play we used last year that worked so well? How did I teach that?

As a coach, Swen Nater initially struggled in preparing his practice plans until he recalled the effective and efficient practices he participated in at UCLA under the guidance of Coach Wooden.

I remembered saving some daily practice plans. If I could find enough of them, I could fill in the missing pieces and have the start of a year-long plan. I leafed frantically through my files. I thought I had the information I needed in a file folder, which I yanked out of the drawer and opened as if it was a Christmas gift. But fragments were all I found, leaving me to question why I threw all of last year's practice plans away?

Every practice my first year had been a learning experience, mostly a lesson on how not to do something. But I did not keep systematic notes, so all I had for my second year were some vague memories of what did and didn't work very well. Part of the problem was my method for creating daily practice plans—it was not quite "winging it," but it was close. Each morning that first year, I spent an hour planning for practice that day. I would start by reflecting on the previous practice and what parts of our game needed more work, and end by allotting time for each activity, based on my best guess for how long each activity would take. The daily lessons had little or no connection to the weekly and yearly plan I had briefly sketched before fall practice began, and had quickly abandoned as I switched to day-to-day, ad hoc practice planning.

Each morning that first year, I'd start out thinking, "We need a little of that and a little of this. We should do this again and that again. How are we doing on the zone offense? Yes, I need to work on that a little because the first game is only one week away." I sometimes lost track of what I had already taught and what still needed to be taught. I was operating day to day, with little regard for yesterday or tomorrow, and that's the way it went every day, every week.

The result? At some point in the early games, the opponent would present some challenge and I would sit on the bench, rolling my fingers over my hair, asking in frustration, "Why did we not work on that?" My team was behind (in knowledge) all season. We were never fully prepared for any contest. My planning had deteriorated into learning from game mistakes and working on them the next practice. I hated this ad hoc approach. I was teaching by putting out fires, not by preparing my team. In a very real way, I was teaching to the weekly test, not to a coherent basketball curriculum. At the end of the season, I looked back in frustration and disappointment, realizing that I had not taught nearly all the required curriculum. I had not prepared the team.

As I sat preparing for my second year, I realized there was no recourse other than to start from scratch. Selecting a fresh legal pad and taking pencil in hand, I began to create a teaching plan, a basketball curriculum for the entire season. It took days, and creating a season plan was only part of the job. Weekly plans had to be made as well as one for the first day of practice. As I labored over my plan, my thoughts drifted back to the practices Coach Wooden ran when I was a player. I realized those lessons at UCLA bore little resemblance to the ones I conducted in my first year. Bill Walton once described our practices this way:

"Practices at UCLA were nonstop, electric, supercharged, intense, demanding … with Coach pacing the sidelines like a caged tiger, barking instructions, positive reinforcement, and maxims: 'Be quick, but don't hurry.' He constantly changed drills and scrimmages, exhorting us to 'move quickly, hurry up.' Games seemed like they happened in a slower gear. I'd think in games, 'why is this taking so long,' because everything we did in games happened faster in practice."[1]

Each one of Coach Wooden's practice sessions were planned to the minute. Every activity lasted a predetermined amount of time, and time was never compromised, for any activity or for the duration of the session. Not a moment was wasted. When the whistle blew, signaling the end of a drill, players, coaches, and managers moved purposefully and quickly to the next drill in a machine-like manner. But there was quickness, not hurrying. Even before we were in place for the next activity, Coach was already shouting instructions. Seniors and experienced team members echoed his instructions to the rest of us. Efficiency, intensity, industriousness, and purpose dominated and controlled our effort and concentration.

He never let up. From the beginning to the end of practice, Coach commanded, exhorted, and demanded our best. He moved with us, around us, before us, and paced, stopped, and started, always setting the pace of practice and constantly increasing the tempo. Although off the court he was a mild-mannered man, when he stepped into his basketball classroom, he was an intense, very verbal, and possessed teacher who had three things on his mind—improvement, improvement, improvement. And off the court, that meant planning, planning, planning.

I also remember that each practice session had a purpose and was related to the one before, the one yet to come, and to some future goal. What we learned was cumulative, like a well-planned math curriculum where prior information was needed to solve future problems.

I began to wonder how Coach Wooden developed such an exhaustive and meticulous plan that resulted in total preparation and the complete domination of men's college basketball. These same questions puzzled others.

Two researchers of pedagogical methods observed almost an entire season of Coach Wooden's practices and noticed the organization, efficiency, and especially the method of instruction.[2] They wondered how he did it. From a variety of sources, including interviews with Coach and from his writings, a picture began to emerge, and it became evident that "proper planning" was key.

Coach Wooden devoted at least two uninterrupted hours per morning to creating a well thought-out plan for every practice. He spent more time on lesson planning than anything else. He kept records of every practice, complete with notes for improvement, and constantly referred to them as he developed and improved practice plans for each season.

"I would spend almost as much time planning a practice as conducting it. Everything was planned out each day. In fact, in my later years at UCLA I would spend two hours every morning with my assistants organizing that day's practice sessions (even though the practice itself might be less than two hours long). I kept a record of every practice session in a loose-leaf notebook for future reference. Prior to practice time, the secretary would type the entire daily plan onto a 3 x 5 index card, gave them to me, and I distributed them to all coaches and managers. Those cards informed every staff member of all activities and the exact time each would start and finish. As a result, coaches and managers were prepared to quickly transition from activity to activity without any wasted time. Every second is important ...

"I could go back to the [19]48-49 year and tell you what we did on November the 15th—minute by minute what we did—and I think that helped me tremendously by doing those [plans]."[3]

Examples of the practice plans summarized on 3 x 5 cards were presented in *Practical Modern Basketball.*

3:30-3:40	Easy running floor length, change of pace and direction, defensive sliding, one on one (cutter), one on one (dribbler), inside turn reverse to receive pass, reverse turn and drive with imaginary ball, jumping.
3:40-3:45	Five man-Rebounding and passing.
3:45-3:50	Five man-Dribble and pivot.
3:50-4:00	Five man-Alternative post pass and cut options.
4:00-4:15:	Three-man lane with one and two men alternating on defense, parallel lane, weave pivot, front and side.[4]

As a result of his detailed planning, Coach Wooden was prepared each and every day to attend to the team's and every individual's immediate instructional needs—and ready to provide tailored instruction accordingly. These included what part of the offense the team and an individual player needed to work on, which moves a particular player needed to perfect at his position, the number of consecutive made free throws required of an individual before he could return to the scrimmage, and many other areas.

For Coach Wooden, each day is an opportunity to create a masterpiece. No minute should be wasted and improvement, even if it's just slight, must be made in every area. While teaching high school English, he learned a valuable lesson—yearly planning and detailed lesson plans maximized student learning. Every minute was important and deserved to be valued and used properly.

According to Coach, planning is planning, whether it's done on the court or in the classroom. He always says he learned how to teach basketball in the high school classroom. But that connection had to be learned. *I knew a detailed plan was necessary in teaching English, but it took a while before I understood the same thing was necessary in sports. Otherwise, you waste an enormous amount of time, effort, and talent.*[5] The result? Every basketball lesson for each practice, week, and season was meticulously fashioned just as a sculptor creates a masterpiece of art.

Planning his English curriculum was not easy at first for Coach Wooden. His first few years as a teacher were filled with trial and error, not unlike most beginning teachers. He noted his inefficiencies and set out to make improvements by seeking out assistance from gifted teachers.

Early in his career, he had the opportunity to observe a football practice at the University of Notre Dame when the legendary Frank Leahy was head coach.

"I thought my basketball practices were well-organized and efficient. After observing Coach Leahy's practice, I realized more work was needed. There was not one minute wasted. Even the transitions from drill to drill were done with no wasted second. Players seemed to enjoy the work and everyone worked hard for the entire two hours. I was impressed and after meeting with Frank Leahy for answers to questions I had, I immediately applied what I had learned to my own situation."[6]

After witnessing Leahy conduct practice so efficiently, Coach Wooden raised the bar for himself and he was determined to jump over it. He continued to learn and to improve his planning. He deeply believes that the teacher and coach *"who has the ability to properly plan ... from both the daily and the long-range point of view together with the ability to devise the necessary drills to meet his particular needs for maximum efficiency has tremendously increased his possibility of success."*[7] Fortunately for all of us, his approach to planning is something he has spoken and written about in detail so that others can learn from his success. The following includes Coach Wooden's method of planning and preparation.

Plan for the Year

Sometime during the off-season, usually late summer when recruiting was finished and Coach Wooden knew what the talent would be that particular year, he wrote his yearly plan for teaching. It was not a chronological plan; it simply contained a number of notes—bullet points about the team and what it needed to learn that season. In a real sense it was the general curriculum for the year.

For example, the 1971-72 "Walton Gang" was relatively new to the system, albeit, as freshmen, Walton, Wilkes, and others ran an offensive and defensive system very similar to what they were going to learn as varsity players. Nevertheless, Coach, aware of some skills already acquired, made a list of what this very young team—myself included—had to learn, pretty much from scratch. He had not been the freshmen's teacher yet, so he assumed they knew nothing. The full-court press; a resurrected half-court offense, used by Lew Alcindor's squad; and a dynamic half-court defense, designed around the exceptional defensive ability of Walton, all had to be taught from the ground up. Therefore, Coach Wooden's yearly plan included such entries as:

- Significant time given to fundamentals.
- Determine if the full-court press or the half-court defense will be the primary defense.
- Develop an outstanding fast break by working Walton and the guards together on the outlet pass and getting the ball out of the back court quickly and safely.

- Develop a half-court offense that utilizes the passing and scoring ability of Walton and the high-post scoring ability of Wilkes. We'll be able to run more plays this year so spend time on a variety of fitting offensive plays using Walton as the hub.
- Find out how to use Bibby's shooting ability to maximum advantage.[8]

For more experienced teams such as the one Coach had the previous year, a different yearly prescription was written. Because many regulars returned to the team, Coach Wooden had a different challenge on his hands—taking an experienced group coming off an NCAA championship year to a higher level, knowing they were already well-grounded in the fundamentals and well-versed in the offensive and defensive system. His yearly plan for this veteran team consisted of:

Find a way to help Steve Patterson [high-post center whose offensive role was limited because of the extreme talent of the forwards, Wicks and Rowe] develop more one-on-one moves and scoring opportunities.

- Introduce two or three more options to get Wicks the basketball in the post.
- Devise plays to get Wicks the basketball on the perimeter for one-on-one end-of-game opportunities.
- Develop Wicks' press defense so players at the front of the full-court press can gamble a little more.
- Improve perimeter shooting because defenses will key on Wicks and Rowe inside.[9]

Plan for the Week

The weekly plan was more specific and detailed and focused on two segments: The preseason and the season. The format was very much the same as the yearly plan.

Preseason Weekly Plan

The preseason curriculum contained every component needed to prepare the team for the first league game. A general overall plan was written that contained everything to be taught and then divided up into weeks. For example, the first week contained more conditioning and fundamental work than offensive and defensive plays, as well as the basic structure of the fast break. The second week, Coach Wooden may have introduced one series of offensive half-court plays, the foundation of the half-court defense, and the foundation of the full-court press. The third week, out-of-bounds plays, more offensive and defensive options, and increased complexity in the full-court press may have been worked on, among other items.

The last week of preseason—the week before the first league game—the jump ball and specific offensive and defensive strategies may have been taught, in preparation for the particular teams we were going to play that weekend.

Also included in the preseason weekly plan were offensive and defensive plays Coach Wooden considered using against particular conference teams. Plays worked on during a particular week were tried against a preseason opponent that weekend and then evaluated for improvement. Those that needed more refinement were strategically inserted into a future weekly plan.

Season Weekly Plan

Weekly plans, beginning with one week prior to the first league game and ending the week of the Final Four, looked more like a planned weekly calendar. In those days, especially during league play, game days were almost always Fridays and Saturdays. That made for a Monday through Thursday weekly practice plan.

Mondays—
- Complimentary remarks and constructive criticism to those who played
- Individual work for those needing improvement in certain areas
- More warm-up since players had one day off
- Shooting
- Introduce new options not used previous weekend
- Extra scrimmage for those who did not see much playing time

Tuesday—
- More of same but more running and scrimmaging

Wednesday—
- Individual Work
- Breakdown of offense
- Five-on-five offense
- Further develop new options introduced on Monday
- Three-on-two conditioner drill
- Full-court controlled scrimmage
- Free-throw shooting

Thursday—
- Fundamentals
- Shooting (game shots)
- Review and stress important points of full-court defensive plan
- Brush up on important defensive points relative to upcoming games
- Review set and out-of-bounds plays
- Lots of free-throw shooting[10]

Carefully scripted daily, weekly, and season lesson plans were crafted by Coach Wooden, who also was actively involved in each practice
session.

Daily Lesson Plans and the Organization of Instruction

*"There are so many things that are extremely important in coaching [and
teaching] ... that I continually find myself referring to one particular idea as,
perhaps, the most important. However, there are many things that must be
emphasized and proper planning of the practice session is one of those."*[11]

For Coach Wooden, planning a week of English instruction was no different
than planning a week of basketball practice. The weekly plan included everything to be taught that week. But Coach's next task was to arrange five lesson
plans (one week) out of the weekly plan. Using the previous two years' three-
ring notebooks, which contained lesson plans, as his guide, he carefully and
deliberately developed the daily plans, paying meticulous attention to applying the following principles.

1. Fundamentals Before Creativity

Webster defines "fundamental" as "being an essential part of, a foundation
or basis." The fundamentals of basketball are the essential skills that make up
the game. Shooting, dribbling, passing, balance, cutting, rebounding, and piv-

oting are all fundamentals of basketball, and each of these have fundamentals of their own. For example, some of the fundamentals of shooting are keeping the ball at chest level and elbows close to the body, fingertip control, quickness, proper position of the elbow, arch, and movement of the head.

Coach Wooden believes the teaching of fundamentals, until they are all executed quickly, properly, and without conscious thought, is prerequisite to playing the game. Drills must be created so that all of the fundamentals are taught to the criterion that players execute them automatically. With a strong foundation, the players are able to play the game effectively, without error.

"Drill" can have a negative connotation among coaches and classroom teachers. It is sometimes associated with mindless, boring repetition in which there is no opportunity for students to learn concepts or exercise initiative or imagination. In Coach Wooden's case, the term "drill" does indeed refer to making execution automatic, but it also means more. He designed lessons so that players could execute the fundamentals so well that they were able to, as the opportunity presented itself, take initiative and exercise imagination. *"Drilling created a foundation,"* he likes to say, *"on which individual initiative and imagination can flourish."*[12] For example, the success of any offensive play is dependent on quick and proper execution of passes, dribbles, cuts, and shots. Drilling in these basic building blocks of team play eventually resulted in automaticity—performing them without conscious thought. This freed players' minds to concentrate and respond creatively and spontaneously to whatever the opposing team tried to do.

The proper rebounding technique involves footwork, the proper position of the hands, a particular mental state, jumping, and timing. All of these things were taught individually and later combined to create the entire act of rebounding from start to finish. Through repetition, the movement became second nature; the player did not need to be conscious of the footwork, hands, etc. When that state of automaticity was achieved, the player was free to concentrate on using creativity to try new things to get to the basketball, offensively and defensively. Rebounding, then, became a part of the game. In a real sense, the game of basketball was taught from the inside-out, with automaticity gained at each level.

This concept is much like the process of reading. Once the fundamentals (i.e., segmentation of sounds, blending of sounds, quick retrieval of sounds from graphemes, multi-syllable decoding strategy, and morphological problem solving) are automatic, the reader is free to concentrate completely on word recognition, prosody, speed, and comprehension. Teaching a child to read out loud with fluency and good expression before the basics is the equivalent of introducing second graders to Macbeth before they've learned Billy Goats Gruff (see chapters 6 and 7 for more on these issues).

2. Use Variety

One of the many enjoyable things I remember about UCLA practice sessions was the variety. Although the general skeleton of practice lessons were the same (fundamentals, break-down drills, and then whole-team activities), there were lots of surprises that kept things interesting and fun.

First, from practice to practice, Coach Wooden rearranged the order of drills. The same activities were part of the practice plan, but he believed in changing the order from time to time.

Second, he also employed variety by creating extensions from basic activities. Extensions were drills that taught, or reinforced the same information, but in a different way, and often with increased complexity and difficulty. *"I must know as the season progressed how they (drills) were going to change,"* he said, *"and then devise new ones to prevent monotony, although there would be some drills we must do every single day of the year."*[13]

Some teachers hopelessly attempt to remember some fun and effective drill or lesson they used years ago. Coach never forgot one of them because he kept a record in a three-ring binder of every lesson plan for every year. Through consulting the previous year's binder, complete with every lesson plan, activity, and improvement suggestions, effective extensions were never lost but frequently resurrected, reused, and improved.

Third, variety was also employed by giving each practice session a theme. From day to day, we never knew what part of the game would be featured. But the theme connected activities and made practice more enjoyable and meaningful because we understood how each drill fit with the others. This is the hallmark of a well-thought out curriculum in which the scope and sequence of concepts is organized and presented in a way that the whole body of knowledge "makes sense" to the students, who can then connect each part of what they are learning.

3. Teaching New Material

When creating the daily lesson plan, Coach Wooden was careful to install new material in the first half of practice, not the second. There were two reasons for this: our minds were fresh and not yet worn down by two hours of high-intensity activities, and he could devise activities, during the second half of practice, for the application of the new material. For example, early in practice Coach Wooden introduced a new option for the offense, perhaps one we needed to execute during one of the upcoming weekend games. He began with detailed explanations and demonstrations of all moves, passes, and shots. When it was our turn to run the play, our efforts were met with a bombardment of his corrections, reproofs and, at times, lack of patience. In short, as we ran the play again and again, through the mental pressure he administered, it began to take form.

The majority of the second half of practice was reserved for controlled full-court scrimmage. During this segment Coach Wooden planned for us to apply the new play to game conditions. We were not learning anything new; we were applying what Coach had introduced and, through repetition and pressure, perfecting it at game speed. Just as in the classroom, it is essential that new learning be woven into the fabric of existing knowledge through practice and application. When the process is complete there is no longer a seam distinguishing the new from the old, and the body of knowledge and skill that the students command has grown in volume, texture, and value.

4. Quick Transitions

During Coach Wooden's practice sessions, one witnessed lightning-quick transitions from activity to activity. Players sprinted to the next area and took pride in being the first to begin the next activity. In the first few weeks of the season, those transitions were rather clumsy. In time, however, the movement resembled a fine-tuned machine. For example, at certain intervals we were to move to various baskets to practice free throws (just after completing a strenuous drill, so we were winded, a situation we might confront at the end of a close game). When the whistle blew, every player sprinted to where we were assigned (in advance), to begin shooting. Transitions were as intense as the activities. No time was wasted. But in addition to players sprinting to their new spots, those transitions were quick and economical because managers, who were given a copy of the practice plan, had all necessary equipment at the appropriate locations ready when the changeover occurred.

Classroom teachers can decrease the time and energy needed to change from one activity to another by doing the same. Of course, no managers are available to help but volunteers can be recruited from sources such as local businesses, graduate students, and the retired. Or, students who excel can be given leadership roles in this area. Notebooks, textbooks, pencils, erasers, and other materials needed for the next activity can be quickly placed in position or handed out toward the end of the previous activity's conclusion. In short, with a little ingenuity, creativity, and organization, classrooms can be morphed from inefficient operations to efficient systems.

5. Increasing Complexity

For Coach Wooden, there was nothing more important than the fundamentals of the game. The development of a firm foundation was the priority and that meant the quick and proper execution of the basics of basketball.

At the beginning of the year, lesson plans contained activities that would teach only one fundamental at a time, but quickly evolved to activities that focused primarily on one fundamental while also including other fundamentals that had already been learned but required repeated practice. For example, initially shooting and dribbling forms were isolated. Then, Coach taught another type of dribbling technique and combined it so that a shot was taken after the dribble. Fundamentals were carefully sequenced so combinations could be created, first two, then three, then four fundamentals in one drill. Drills evolved from simple to extremely complex and demanding. Every movement, every action was carefully thought out and planned.

6. Conditioning

At first glance, conditioning would seem to have little relevance to the class-room. But it does. Visit a school early in the academic year, and you will see children who are out of "classroom learning" condition. Attention spans have been summer-trained to be short and focus only on what is entertaining—television, video games, and kinesthetic activities. Kindergarten and preschool teachers know that children, who have been conditioned to sit and listen to someone read, are able to do so when they enter school.

Taking into account students' "classroom conditioning" was something Coach Wooden practiced when he taught English, and something he considered when planning. Early in the year, less time was spent on activities, and more time on explanation; mental demands were less and intensity was lower. Just as on the practice floor, each succeeding day saw incremental elevation in expectations, activity duration and demands. Activities were included and arranged so that the proper level of mental and emotional conditioning challenge would be supplied at all times, resulting in sustained improvement.

Applying the same concept to basketball resulted in UCLA's basketball team usually being considered the best-conditioned team in the nation every season. There was something mysterious and awesome about a group of athletes whose physical and mental conditioning was nearly flawless, even during the last minutes of a game. But, when early season practice sessions started, we were not close to that level. Mental, emotional, and physical condition had to be developed.

Coach Wooden's philosophy is for players and students to improve a little every day and make perfection the goal. His method for improving condition-ing included one painful demand—each player, when reaching the point of exhaustion, was to push himself beyond. When this is done every day, top con-dition will be attained over time. To accomplish this, he started with practices that were moderately demanding (or at least that was his opinion) and increased the demands a little each day. The first two weeks of practice were one-half hour longer than those later on in the year, but during those early ses-sions more time was given to explanation, drills were shorter in duration, fewer drills were severely demanding, and there were more breaks. As the days pro-gressed, the daily lesson plans changed, containing two or more demanding activities in succession, longer duration for activities, and less recess. This effec-

Coach Wooden valued his preparation time with his assistants so much that interruptions were not allowed during that designated time period.

tive system developed gradual conditioning without increasing the chance for injury, which often happens when physical demands are too strong, too early.

Whether in the classroom or on the court, conditioning is important and can be developed and improved. Imagine an entire classroom full of students who can work and learn for a complete school day, day after day. Can it be done? Yes, one step at a time. Carefully constructed lesson plans can make it a reality.

7. End on a Positive Note

I remember many enjoyable endings to the UCLA practice sessions. Coach Wooden always had something interesting, challenging, or fun planned for the last five minutes. I didn't realize it at the time, but levity always helped bring me back the next day, filled with anticipation.

During my time at UCLA, dunking was not allowed in games and therefore it was prohibited in practice. However, on one occasion, a player dunked the basketball over another and all of us began to laugh (after the initial shock and a look over to Coach Wooden to see how he reacted). To our surprise, he didn't say anything until five minutes to go in practice.

"So you fellows get a kick out of dunking the basketball, do you?" he asked, raising his voice. *"You know that it's not allowed in games and that is exactly why I don't allow it,"* he said, raising his voice even more. But then he suddenly smiled and, speaking softly, said, *"But I will let you get it out of your system just this once. Every one will have one chance to dunk. We'll decide who is the best."*

What a tease! We thought he was angry. Dunking, cheering, clapping, and laughing, we had the time of our lives for four minutes, while Coach Wooden just stood, with folded arms, smiling and chuckling. Needless to say, we couldn't wait for the next practice to begin. It was another great one.

8. Avoid Altering a Plan During the Lesson

Once the practice, or lesson, started, Coach Wooden never changed it, even though he may have noticed an existing drill that needed more time or thought of a new one he should have included. The proper place for new ideas and improvements was on the back of the 3 x 5 index card, which he made notations on (and expected the assistants to do the same). After practice, the coaching staff would review all of the notes taken and decisions were made for future planning purposes, especially for the next day's workout. Most of the notes concerned devising new methods to improve the play of certain, key individuals. Those ideas were discussed during the following day's practice plan session. But during practice, Coach was reluctant to introduce *ad hoc* changes. He believed that more often than not such hasty changes in the plan would lead to more problems. He thought it was better to keep notes, and plan an effective instructional response after there was time to think it through. In this regard, he was practicing something researchers have found—that effective teachers take time to anticipate specific student difficulties and design instruction to meet them. But unless that is done carefully, students may become more confused.

Another concern he had was the possibility of extending practice through ad hoc changes. He strongly believed in ending practices on time; otherwise players might hold back, anticipating a need for energy reserves if the practice was extended. Because we knew practice would stop promptly at 5:29 p.m. without exception, he felt he could maintain the intensity level throughout the session and we would be willing to extend ourselves, knowing exactly when the exertion would end.

During my first year of coaching, I violated this principle almost every practice session. I would add time to a drill I thought needed more attention. I subtracted time from drills I believed we had mastered. I injected a drill I thought I should have included in the plan. The result was a mess. When I lengthened practice, the players did not work and concentrate as hard. When I added something but kept practice the same length, it took away from something important.

Time Management and Organization

Coach has a very simple approach to time-management—priorities. At the top of the list was setting *consistent, sufficient,* and *uninterrupted* time aside for planning the practice session. He was a man of organization and planning. *"Failure to prepare is preparing to fail,"* he preached many times and practiced always. Although there were many demands for his time, he never ever let any other commitment interfere with his sacrosanct planning time for the practice session. He always practiced this principle while at UCLA, and he always practiced it as a high school English teacher. Those two hours were the most sacred hours of the day (other than family time, which, by the way, was also planned for).

On a January day in 1973, at 9:00 in the morning, as a UCLA student, I entered the athletic department building where the basketball coaching staff occupied offices. I wanted to talk to Coach Wooden and went by his office to see if he was available. To my surprise, the door was closed, so I knocked. There was no answer. I knew he was in there because I heard voices, but no one came to answer my petition.

Plan B for me was to see the secretary and see if she would place a call into Coach Wooden's office and tell him that I wanted to see him. I approached the secretary and presented my request. Her eyes opened as wide as the Grand Canyon and, with all the empathy but seriousness she could muster, she said, "Swen, apparently you don't know this, but at this time in the morning the coaching staff prepares for practice and, unless we're having an earthquake or something, there are no interruptions by anyone."

While I understood this, I asked her, jokingly, "And if Mr. Morgan (the prominent UCLA athletic director) were to ask you to call him?"

"The same applies for him as for everyone else in this world," she said with a confident smirk. "No one disturbs his most sacred time—practice planning."

Although I was young, and my time-management experience was limited to setting my alarm clock, getting to class, allowing time for ping pong and pool, and reserving valuable time for cramming the night prior to exams, I understood that day a little better what time-management was—it had to do with priorities. Although Coach Wooden loved me, during practice planning time, talking to me was not the priority.

Coach learned early in his career how important time management was. Fresh out of Purdue University and a two-year stint as a teacher and coach at

Dayton (Kentucky) High School, he took a teaching position at Central High School, in South Bend, Indiana. But four classes of English per day was only a fraction of his responsibilities. He was the school's athletic director and also coached basketball, baseball, and tennis. He was asked to coach the football team as well but, having little knowledge and no experience with the sport, he convinced the principal to allow the ex-coach to resume the position. Coach Wooden did, however, assist the head coach in football. Later, at Indiana State, Wooden was the university's athletic director, head basketball coach, head baseball coach, and a freshman English instructor.

Many years later, when taking the head basketball coaching position at UCLA, and having a much lighter workload, the time-management skills he learned while overloaded at Central High School and Indiana State paid great dividends. Someone once said, "If you want something done well, give it to a busy person." Busy people learn how to manage their time, or else they'll burn out, fail, or do both.

What were Coach Wooden's principles for time-management? There were three.

Priority

Practice planning was a sacred time. It was always at the same time of day, in the morning, and was never interrupted except for emergencies. As loving, kind, considerate, and friendly as Coach was, all of his players and assistant coaches had the wisdom not to "mess" with his priorities. Priorities were given priority. He had an unbending commitment to the most important things in his life and he knew that managing his time would ensure that the things closest to his heart would receive the proper time. Away from UCLA that was faith, family, and friends. At work it was planning, practice, and then everything else.

Pattern

Consistency is a major key to time-management. Search for and discover the best time to do planning, and do your planning at that same time every day. When the priorities receive their own place in the day, each day will have the same pattern. Pattern begets comfort and productivity.

Patience

An abundance of patience is needed to manage time consistently. Making the change to becoming a good time-manager may be very difficult. There will be times when the teacher realizes that there are errors in the schedule, such as not enough time given to a math activity or that two mentally taxing activities were placed back-to-back. Also, because managing time completely may result in other staff members confusing organization for indifference, misunderstandings may surface. The rest of the staff may not be as organized or time-managed. This teacher may have to adjust things, but should never compromise the time needed for the most important things (priorities).

In the long run, time management will save time and make teachers more productive. As odd as it may sound, the time spent on planning, no matter how long it takes, will save time in the end and result in organization and productivity. The teacher will see the difference, but as Coach Wooden has said, *"It will take faith and patience."*

Planning and Classroom Teachers: A Cautionary Tale

The contrast was stunning. The two middle school classrooms, Room 120 and Room 121, were side-by-side. Outside, from the hallway, they looked exactly the same. The doors were identical, yet inside, there was a stark difference in management and activity.

Room 121 was chaotic. It was difficult for an observer to tell, but there was a history lesson going on in the room. Papers were lying all over the floor. The teacher's desk was covered with paperwork. The students had moved the desks around so they would be able to talk to each other. Incessant talking and arguing was taking place. What was most bothersome, however, was what happened next. The instructor hurried to his desk, which was at the rear of the room, and looked at a piece of paper (which was the schedule for the day) and said, "OK class. We've gone 10 minutes over on the history lesson. We'll have to cut the social studies time down a little today. Put away your history books and please get out your social studies book now."

Room 120 was organized. Everything was in its place. There was no trash on the floor, the desks were all straight, and the children were quietly working. I waited long enough to hear something I have rarely heard in a classroom—the sound of a timer. Simultaneously, the teacher said in a pleasant voice, "Time for math." To my surprise, the children put old materials away, stored them, and retrieved their mathematics materials. In a matter of seconds, even before the teacher worked her way to the front of the classroom, they were prepared. Each transition was quick and efficient, even transitions from an activity to recess and back. And the system for transitioning from lunch back to the classroom was a masterpiece. All students were prepared to enter the classroom as a unit and had made preparation for the second half of the school day by using the lavatory.

At the end of the day, I approached the door of Room 120 and turned the handle. The teacher was alone, sitting at her desk and looked up. "May I help you?" she asked.

"Yes, I would love to talk to you a few minutes," I requested. "I have some questions about how you run your class. I am impressed."

Coach Wooden, pictured here with assistant coach Eddie Powell, learned to budget his time wisely while serving as the athletic director, head basketball coach, head baseball coach, and a freshman English instructor at Indiana State University.

Confidently, but respectfully, the teacher said, "I would love to talk but I can't now because I'm planning my lesson for tomorrow. How much time do you need?"

"About 15 minutes," I answered.

She looked at a calendar and asked, "Can you meet at lunch tomorrow?"

I said that I could and as I closed the door, I noticed the teacher logging our appointment in her calendar. The next day at lunch, all my questions were answered in less than 15 minutes. The answer to her success was very clear. The difference was "time management." As this teacher demonstrated by not allowing me to interrupt her most precious planning time (which, by the way was 90 minutes), her secret was in making sure that the most important things received the proper amount of time.

Conclusion

As the story of Room 120 reveals, planning is just as important for classroom teachers as it is for coaches. In fact, the stakes are higher. If my players don't learn, we might lose games and put a successful season at risk. When my mathematics and reading students don't learn, their academic careers are in jeopardy. The incomplete and unconnected planning I did my first season was not all that unusual. A lot of beginning teachers spend at least their early years experimenting, using the trial and error approach. There is nothing wrong with this method, but starting from scratch every year is self-defeating. Reinventing the wheel every year is frustrating and can extinguish a teacher's spirit. Equally important, precious time that should have been devoted to learning is forever lost.

With few exceptions, most teachers want their students to learn, meet, and even exceed curriculum standards. In recent times, many report they are encountering pressure to meet new and higher curriculum standards. It seems the pressure will become only greater in the coming decades. In 2001, new federal legislation and state testing standards have added new challenges and pressures to already overloaded job requirements.[14] Soon, schools (and teachers) will be accountable for Annual Yearly Progress (AYP). Schools must attain a predetermined AYP or suffer consequences. Those schools that fail their AYP target may be reorganized, and the faculty and administration replaced. By 2014, every student must be proficient in basic skills and knowledge.[15] Win-loss records, so it would seem, will become as common a measure of performance for schools as it is for coaches.

The expectation to achieve yearly progress is something coaches know all about. Depending on the school, the standard can be the national championship, the state championship, the league championship, or simply improvement. From the professional to high school ranks, every year, coaches are fired for not meeting these expectations. In some cases, standards are very high while in others, they are not as demanding. Some athletic directors set clear and measurable standards while others imply them. But in almost every case, the job of the coach is to produce a winner and those who don't will face the consequences.

Thus, time management is as crucial in schools as it was to the success of Coach Wooden's UCLA teams. One study found that efforts to improve instruction often failed because times set aside for teachers to work together were preempted for non-instructional matters, or the meetings simply never happened though they were on the school calendar.[16] When time devoted to instructional planning and improvement was held sacred, within two years schools were able to significantly improve instruction, resulting in much better student achievement. The key is teachers in grade levels and departments meeting regularly to focus on common student needs, planning and implementing alternative instruction, and routinely examining student work to locate areas of continuing need and identify effective re-instruction. These are all very simple tasks, but they are very difficult to do in any school lacking coherence and continuity for teachers to work on improving instruction. And that is what time management is—coherence and continuity—scheduling a time to meet, plan, and work (and following through) by giving each task a necessary amount of time and giving the priorities priority.

A key to successful, effective teaching, whether on the court or in the classroom, is careful and thorough planning based on learning from successes and failures and then making improvements. The perfect yearly, weekly, and daily plans will not be created during a teacher's first year in the classroom. I, for one, can give testimony to that fact. But by using each year's plan as a reference point to make improvements for the following year and continuously evaluating the plans and one's practices, substantial and progressive improvements will be manifested day after day, week after week, and year after year.

Coach Wooden placed high value on time. He made the effort to make each day a masterpiece and that meant he never wanted to waste a minute. That kind of lofty objective required careful planning and determination to become a reality. For Coach Wooden, it did.

In my second year of teaching basketball, I stuck with the yearly, weekly, and daily lesson plans. Motivated by the promise that planning would eliminate failure, my daily lesson plans were based on the weekly plan and the weekly plans on the yearly. In addition, I kept copious notes during practices, applied them to future sessions for improvement and never changed a practice plan once it was initiated. It was a painful procedure for me and temptation to relapse haunted me daily, but my faith prevailed. The struggle was worth it. I believe the team reached its full potential that year and was prepared for every contest.

The Laws of Learning

At the start of all your teaching,
You would show me what to do;
Always leading by example,
Demonstration of "how to."

Then you'd say, "Now you must try it;
I have shown you how to be."
Imitation—I attempted,
As you watched me lovingly.

"Do it this way. Do it that way.
Try it once again like this."
Your correction drilling habit,
As we watched my skills progress.

With occasional assistance,
You retreated humbly.
You were finished—I had learned it.
Repetition was the key.

Swen Nater

Chapter 6

The Laws of Teaching and Learning:
John Wooden's Pedagogy

By the time I arrived at UCLA, John Wooden was almost 60 years of age. Through his own research and development system, he had acquired knowledge about basketball and teaching seldom matched, and probably never surpassed. Having already won six national titles (four in a row), he was in the midst of completing the most astonishing achievement in the history of intercollegiate athletics—winning seven national titles in succession, and 10 in 12 years.

As a novice student, I entered Coach Wooden's classroom at the point when he had nearly perfected his pedagogy. The instruction I received reflected what he had learned about teaching from 38 years of practice. But, as he would quickly add, he was still learning and did so through his final year of teaching.

John Wooden's Pedagogical Approach

A key goal of Coach Wooden was the development of players who were creative, confident problem-solvers. He taught that it is the opponents that determine a team's responses during a game. He wanted us to be so automatic in our basketball fundamentals and so versed in the concepts that we were ready to quickly devise our own solution methods for the constantly changing problems our opponents posed.

As games progress, opponents change how they play defense or offense, presenting new problems by taking away what is working and trying to force the other team to play in a way it might not want to. In response to these changes,

Coach Wooden wanted *"to be as surprised as our opponent at what my team came up with when confronted with an unexpected challenge."*[1]

A basketball player who had learned to automatically execute a specific offensive maneuver might be successful as long as the opponent fails to adjust. But once the other team makes defensive adjustments, the offensive player's success depends on the ability to develop solution methods in response. Coach Wooden's goal was to teach the underlying concepts of offensive and defensive basketball, so that when opponents surprised us with new and different challenges we in turn surprised our coach and the other team with creative and effective solution methods.

To get his players to the point where we surprised him with our innovations, we needed to master two things: (1) grounding in the fundamentals, or basic building blocks of basketball, and (2) mastery of offensive and defensive concepts. The fundamentals—cutting, passing, receiving, dribbling, ball-handling, rebounding, defensive movement, and shooting—needed to be executed with automaticity (i.e., no conscious thought) so attention could be placed on solving the problem and surprising the opponent. For Coach Wooden, the automatic execution of the fundamentals and the understanding of the whole play were non-negotiable prerequisites to making quick and good choices in response to an opponent's changing strategies and tactics. By good choices, of course, he meant choices that remained within his concept of team-oriented play.

The conceptual and problem-solving challenges of high-level collegiate basketball might be more formidable than many fans may realize. For example, offensive plays consist of two simultaneous aspects (execution on the side where the ball is, and execution on the "weak" or non-ball side). The combined actions and responses of five individuals, all happening in a matter of seconds at a rapid pace, determines the outcome of an offensive play. For a play to have a high probability of success, each of the five individuals must understand that the purpose for execution on the ball side (only three of five players at most) is contingent on comprehending the actions of all five. Add multiple options that each individual must select in a flash, each contingent on what the opponents do, and some of the complexity of the basketball curriculum becomes apparent.

To develop his players' capacities to "surprise" him with our solution methods during games, Coach Wooden used a systematic pedagogical approach that he describes as the "whole-part" method.

"I tried to teach according to the whole-part method. I would show them the whole thing to begin with. Then I'm going to break it down into the parts and work on the individual parts and then eventually bring them together. [I wanted to teach] within the framework of the whole, but don't take away the

individuality because different ones are going to have different things at which they excel."[2]

He divided the application of the "whole-part" method into two steps: introducing the concepts (the whole and the parts), and teaching the parts of the whole.

Introducing the Concepts: The Whole-Part Method

Coach Wooden believes it is essential to first show the whole concept of a basketball strategy, or the entire play. With five players on the practice floor, and the rest standing on the sidelines, watching and listening, he carefully explained the purpose of the play and the movement of the basketball and players. Then, when the offense was broken down into its parts by dividing the group into subgroups that worked at different baskets, the purpose of each part—how that part fit into the big picture, the play—became apparent.

Teaching the Parts of the Whole: The Laws of Learning

"There are little details in everything you do, and if you get away from any one of the little details, you're not teaching the thing as a whole. For it is the little things which, together, make the whole. This, I think, is extremely important."[3]

Once he was confident players understood the "whole" concept of a play, the team began working on the parts. It was during those breakdown activities that Coach used what he called "The Laws of Learning" to develop quick and proper team execution. In time, through correction and repetition, the basic movements of the play became automatic and our minds became free to use individual and collective initiative and creativity to solve problems that defenses presented within the flow of a game.

"I think I followed the laws of learning in basketball or baseball or tennis or whatever I taught as far as sports were concerned through the years as much as I did teaching a youngster how to parse a sentence or something in English classes that I taught."[4]

Coach's Laws of Learning are explanation, demonstration, imitation, correction, and repetition, which are clustered together here and described in the following manner: explanation/demonstration, imitation/correction, and repetition.

Explanation/Demonstration

Whenever Coach Wooden taught his players something new, he would first explain and demonstrate. Both are equally important; they are two sides of the same coin. This concept is often overlooked, or at least, depreciated. Teachers are quick to engage students in complex activities without a clear model of

During games, Coach Wooden wanted his players to be innovative, within the team concept, when attempting to solve an opponent's changing strategies and tactics.

what the final product should look like. According to Coach Wooden, a teacher at any level and for any discipline should never take for granted that students understand what to do, or the "big picture" of what they are learning. Explanation alone will usually be insufficient to clearly communicate direction. Coach's demonstrations were extremely thorough and seemed, at the time, to be overkill. Maybe so, but I do know one thing: he seldom had to explain something twice.

Imitation/Correction

As players imitated his model, he and his assistants immediately corrected every error, no matter how small. He would not wait to correct because he believed the context of the correction would be lost unless done immediately. For example, he would not let an error go until the end of a drill, but would shout it out immediately, or halt the activity for a few seconds to deliver the correction.

He and the assistants incessantly shouted small bits of information on how to do drills correctly. When the players got it right, Coach Wooden increased the pace and intensity of the activity. Increased speed led to increased errors, which, consequently, led to more corrections by the coaching staff. In this way, increasing levels of difficulty were reached until the activity was performed at game speed. There is no way to vividly describe the intensity of the process and the "corrections." Suffice it to say, we were pushed to our physical and mental limits, and most of us were convinced that compared to practices the games were relatively easy.

The frequent, short corrections were observed and documented during the 1974-75 season by researchers who observed and recorded Coach Wooden's actions during afternoon practices.[5] They anticipated that it would be difficult to devise a system for counting and reporting his teaching practices. It was not. They encountered none of the messy problems they expected. In fact, it was easy because of the short, punctuated, and numerous corrections that characterized Coach Wooden's teaching. There were no lectures and no extended harangues. None. Not one in all the months they observed. Although frequent and often in rapid-fire order, his comments were so distinct that the researchers were able to code and count each one as a separate event.

To the researchers' surprise, most of Coach's statements in practice were short corrections or statements of how to play basketball. In fact, 75% of everything he said carried information intended for learning. The researchers were surprised at how seldom he positively reinforced players by praising them, or scolded their errors. Years later, Gallimore asked him about this. This is the exchange:

"Of the 2,500 things Roland and I recorded about what you said, most were just plain information about how to play basketball," Gallimore said. "We calculated that 75% of everything you said was information about the proper way to do something in a particular context. We didn't observe you praising or scolding players that much."

"*I believe that [giving lots of information] is the positive approach. I believe in the positive approach.*"[6]

All those short, terse "information-rich" corrections Gallimore and Tharp observed were a positive method of teaching. Instead of haranguing players for making errors, Coach Wooden focused on delivering information players could use to remedy errors and correctly perform what he had previously explained and demonstrated.

Having been the recipient of plenty of corrections, it was the "information" I received in the form of a correction that I needed most. Having received it, I could then make the adjustments and changes needed. It was the information that promoted change. Had the majority of Coach Wooden's corrective strategies been positive ("Good job.") or negative ("No, that's not the way."), I would have been left with an evaluation, not a solution. Also, corrections in the form of information did not address or attack me as a person. New information was aimed at the act, rather than the actor.

Players learned to expect correction for every error, at the time it occurred, no exception. Perfection was the goal and perfection could not be reached unless every error was addressed and rectified. All through practices, Gallimore and Tharp observed him shout corrections such as:

- *"Get your elbow in."*
- *"Follow through."*
- *"Be quick but don't hurry."*
- *"You're too slow. Hustle."*
- *"Goodness, gracious sakes, get the ball to the guard."*
- *"Don't dribble the ball. Pass it."*
- *"That's showmanship. There is no room for that. Play together."*
- *"How many times do I have to show you how to come off the screen? Set yourself up and then make the quick move."*
- *"You're off balance. Your feet should be a little wider than your shoulders, chin up, hands close to your body, and your head should be above the midpoint between your feet. Now do it right."*[7]

Coach Wooden's frequent corrections are in striking contrast to an American teaching practice of mitigating student errors as opposed to capitalizing on them to correct student misunderstanding of crucial concepts.[8] When students made errors in mathematical procedures, typical mitigations by U.S. teachers included: "That's close, you are on the right track, and you were almost there." Although at first glance these mitigations might seem innocuous, Santagata's careful examination of lesson videos revealed something possibly alarming. Instead of identifying and exploring with students any misconceptions that caused procedural errors, American teachers often gave the correct answer or called on students until one provided the correct answer. What the teachers seldom did was spend time analyzing the error to expose the student misunderstanding, and provide corrective instruction. Simply hearing the right answer does not ensure that students who made the computational errors because of a fundamental misunderstanding of the underlying math concepts receives the instruction they need the most. In contrast, Coach Wooden teaches that errors should be identified immediately, and immediately corrected using a variety of instructional moves so that students understand better what they are learning, why, and how each part relates to the whole. He never mitigated an error; he used them to extract for his students the maximum learning benefit.

Employing the "whole-part" method of instruction allowed Coach Wooden to get his players to see how each of their specific duties fit into the grand scheme of every play.

In addition to short, terse corrections, there was another instructional move that distinguished his teaching, one so unique that Tharp and Gallimore called it a *Wooden*.*[9] Nearly 10% of his teaching acts were *Woodens,* which were comprised of three distinct steps: Coach first demonstrated the correct way that an activity was to be performed. Second, he demonstrated how the offender had been in error. Finally, he repeated the correct way to perform.

"Let me show you, Swen. This is how you screen for the player. You pivot on your left foot. Now, here is how you did it. Let me show you how to do it again. Do you understand?" That method of correction took place several times per practice.

After shooting a perimeter shot, players were trained to immediately go into the middle of the key to take the responsibility for the long rebound. Prior to my enrollment at UCLA, I, like the rest of the players, was in the habit of watching my shot after I landed instead of instantly moving to my assigned rebounding position. It would take a computer to keep track of all of the times

* In the research literature on coaching a Wooden might be described as the "sandwich technique" (Tutko & Richards, 1971).

Coach Wooden had to correct this error. I, and most of the other newcomers, really struggled with correcting this habit. Because I had difficulty learning it, and Coach did not want to stop practice every time I made the omission, he would simply shout, *"Go to the key!"* when I landed after shooting. The instruction came so often that I began to hear it even if he didn't say it. And many times, I dreamed of him telling me to *"Go to the key!"*

Repetition

"The teacher must demonstrate and explain, have students imitate while being corrected, and, when the desired performance is obtained, have the student repeat, repeat, and repeat it until it becomes automatic. Explaining and demonstrating the correct model always comes first, and can be repeated whenever necessary, even during the repetition stage. Correction may be needed during the repetition stage as well. Although there are four laws of learning, and the explanation and demonstration starts the process, all four are in operation once the imitation starts. However, the more the student does it correctly, the more the teacher backs off and allows him to gradually become independent. For one fundamental this procedure may be repeated for many days or even weeks before I felt it had become automatic. In fact, we never stopped repetition until the end of the season."[10]

Coach Wooden's last law of learning is Repetition. The purpose of repetition is to develop *automaticity*. He defines automaticity as performing an operation with absolutely no conscious thought of bodily movements. The concept is, when a basketball player has reached this level of development, the physical movements are second nature and total concentration is placed on playing the game and being able to make multiple, instantaneous decisions. A basketball player with automaticity, therefore, is able to fully concentrate on making quick decisions rather than worrying about which hand to dribble with or performing the proper shooting technique.

Repetition begins when students begin to imitate. Repeated correction results in the student performing the task increasingly well. Once the student can perform without much assistance, repetition continues until the habit is second nature.

After UCLA shot the basketball, team offensive rebounding balance was key to obtaining offensive rebounds and for defensive alignment in case the opponent gained possession of the basketball. This configuration included three inside rebounders (near the basket), a long rebounder (just below the free-throw line), and a protector (moving toward the half-court line). As mentioned above, after a player took an outside shot, he became the "long rebounder" and was to immediately move to the area just below the free-throw line. When commencing their UCLA careers, few players performed this maneuver by habit; most just remained where they landed after they shot the basketball.

Breaking the old habit and installing the new took weeks to bring to automaticity. For the first weeks of practice, correcting those who failed to learn was a major coaching task. The drills and incessant barking of all three coaches didn't stop until all players instinctively made this move.

After the last practice of my senior year, the day before the NCAA championship game, an observer of that practice was astounded by the basic drills the team practiced (the same drills we did at the beginning of the season). Offensive success was a key to UCLA's victory in the championship game and many of those offensive rebounds were obtained by the long rebounder. The repetition paid off. Coach Wooden attaches so much importance to repetition that, with a smile, he often says:

"There are actually eight laws of learning—Demonstration, Explanation, Imitation, Repetition, Repetition, Repetition, Repetition, and Repetition. The importance of repetition until automaticity cannot be overstated. Repetition is the key to learning. There is absolutely no substitute for repetition. I believe in learning by repetition to the point where everything becomes automatic ... the best teacher is repetition, day after day, throughout the season."[11]

Putting it All Together

With repetition, supported by explanation, demonstration, imitation, and correction when necessary, the team's improvement accelerated. The more automatic the fundamentals and the movements of the plays became, the more time players had to come up with new and more effective ways to solve problems posed by opponents. For example, automaticity in rebounding and defensive balance helped us come up with creative ways to secure more offensive rebounds and administer instant defensive pressure. Long rebounders learned when they could move in a little closer to the basket or drop back while the protectors found new ways to discourage or steal the long pass.

Though many outsiders thought Coach Wooden was "set in his ways," in reality, he was extremely open to better ways of doing things. One example of his openness to student initiative and creativity occurred when he was a young high school basketball coach. At the time, he was using an offensive strategy that he learned from his previous teachers and other coaches he respected. One of those "truths" concerned the positioning of the tallest player, the center, at the high-post (free-throw line) area when setting a screen for the guard after the guard had passed the ball to the forward at the wing. It was generally accepted that the screener faced toward his teammate and away from the basket. However, being able to see his teammate and his teammate's defender often caused the screener to attempt to assist his teammate a little by leaning

Courtesy of UCLA Photography

Coach Wooden placed so much emphasis on repetition in practice because he believes it is the key to learning.

or sticking an elbow out in order to slow down the defender as he passed. This often resulted in a foul on the tallest player on the floor and a loss of possession of the basketball.

On one occasion, instead of facing away from the basket, the center surprised his coach by turning and facing away from his teammate and toward the basket. The guard, acting as if nothing was out of the ordinary, used his teammate for a screen and, to everyone's surprise, the guard was open. The forward passed him the ball and he scored. After the game, Coach Wooden asked the center why he had turned his back to set the screen, to which the center replied, "I didn't want any more fouls and I figured, if I turned my back so I couldn't see my teammate, I wouldn't get one." Coach commended him for his ingenuity and, from that moment on, taught the reverse pivot and back screen.

The following games and practices revealed two additional benefits to implementing the new technique that were not anticipated. Because the high-post player faced the basket and, therefore, his defender, once or twice every game he was able to surprise his defender by slipping to the basket for a quick catch and score. The second benefit was, because the center's back was turned to his teammate, all of the responsibility for getting free from the defender belonged to the guard. The guard could no longer rely on his teammate to bump his defender. The result was guards who became very skilled at using screens.

Because it was a "truth," the reverse screening position stood the test of time and, along with many other refinements, eventually became part of what was later known as the UCLA high-post offense used by all of Coach Wooden's championship teams in one form or another.

This is just one example that illustrates that Coach Wooden was open to new ideas and creative problem solving. And his players felt the freedom to help him do just that.

"I never wanted to take away their individuality, but I wanted that effort to be put forth to the welfare of the group as a whole. I don't want to take away their thinking. I wanted options. I wanted a second and third option on most of the plays that we would set up and I wanted our plays to come within the framework of our general overall philosophy and not say you have to do this, you have to do this, and you have to do this. I never wanted to take away their individual initiative, but I wanted them to put that to use at the proper time for the welfare of the group."[12]

Conclusion

Repetition and drill have a bad name in some teaching circles. For some, "drill is a way to kill" student interest and learning. For others, it is fundamental to teaching. Some believe skills and drills should always take a back seat to assisting learners to construct meaning and understanding. There is a tendency to regard the two points of view as polar opposites.

Coach Wooden takes a different view. He does not believe teachers have to choose between drill and repetition to achieve automaticity, and teaching that encourages thinking, understanding, and initiative. The former is the servant of the latter, in his view. This idea is not so new to many veteran teachers, but it remains controversial in many education circles.

There is no doubt on this point: Coach Wooden is strong on basic skills, drill, and repetition. He knows the right way, and he sees one of his roles as teaching students to perform skills and fundamentals automatically, a principle that research supports.[13] However, achieving automaticity through repetition is a means to an end for Coach, not the end in itself.

In his pedagogy, drill and repetition are intended to achieve an automaticity or mastery of fundamentals to create a foundation on which individual initiative and imagination can flourish. In the execution of their roles on the court, he wanted to unburden his players from thinking about matters they could leave to automatic performance, in order to free them to think, choose, be inventive and imaginative, and take initiative.

This is parallel to some views in reading instruction. For example, research indicates that fluent readers recognize printed words quickly and almost without thinking—here *fluent* means being able to decode and recognize words with speed, accuracy, and expression. Fluent reading reduces the workload of decoding and recognizing individual words, and allows readers to focus more attention on comprehending what they are reading.[14] In other words, automatic, fluent reading of words is the means to the ends of understanding what is in the book. Like readers, Coach Wooden wanted his players to be fluent in their execution of fundamentals so that they had the mental bandwidth to think about what they were doing.

He also did not teach and practice skills out of context. He always made sure players understood the whole of what they were learning, so that as he introduced and drilled them on the parts, they understood how each related to the whole. Many parts of a practice included a good balance of drill and playing competitive basketball. Thus, while fundamental skills were being practiced, they were in a chunk large enough for players to see their relevance to whole schemes of defense and offense. For example, many drills broke down the offense and defense into one-on-one, two-on-two, three-on-three, four-on-four, and five-on-five situations. These "breakdown" activities were competitive and fun, but Coach Wooden made sure that these parts were eventually understood by players to make up a seamless whole.

There's another interesting parallel, this one between Coach's pedagogy and contemporary views on teaching mathematics. Just as in the case of reading instruction, it is not a perfect analogy because the subject matters are different in fundamental ways. But examining the parallels sharpens appreciation of his approach. Consider Coach Wooden's hope *"to be as surprised as our opponent at what my team came up with when confronted with an unexpected challenge."* The desire to be "surprised" by his players is surprisingly analogous to contemporary ideas on teaching mathematics. If students are only taught to memorize solution methods, any deviation in problem structure or form may stymie them. If they are taught to understand conceptually the underlying mathematics, they are typically better prepared to devise solution methods as the need arises.

"Learning the 'basics' is important; however, students who memorize facts or procedures without understanding often are not sure when or how to use what they know. In contrast, conceptual understanding enables students to deal with novel problems and settings. They can solve problems that they have not encountered before."[15]

Coach Wooden emphasized repetition of fundamentals so that his players would be resourceful, imaginative, and creative, not because he wanted them to be robots mindlessly relying on rote memory. For him, repetition is a means to an end; he firmly believes that when students understand what they are doing and can connect the ideas they are taught, they are better prepared to solve new problems as they arise in the future. He teaches that understanding and conceptual knowledge, supported by automatic mastery of fundamentals, prepares students to tackle problems of all kinds, like those they had encountered before, and novel ones, too. Not only is this an appealing approach to teaching basketball, it is a way to think about teaching all subjects—reading, literature, mathematics, science, and social sciences. As in so many cases outlined in this book, Coach Wooden discovered and used principles and practices worthy of emulation, and as it turns out, consistent with the findings of teaching researchers.

You haven't made a fire till it has burned.
You haven't made a dollar till it's earned.
And no teaching has transpired
If the child has not acquired.
You haven't taught a child till he has learned.

Swen Nater

Chapter 7
You Haven't Taught Until They Have Learned

"You just don't throw material out for someone to get, as I've heard some college professors say. I had a discussion with an English professor at UCLA. We were both asked to go to Sacramento by Dr. Murphy, the Chancellor at UCLA at the time. When we began to discuss teaching, [the professor] indicated that he was there to dispense material and students were to get it. And I said, 'I thought you were there to teach them.' He said, 'No, no, college students should be getting it themselves. Maybe in the lower levels they're taught [but not when they get to the university level].' And I said, 'Well, I think you're always teaching.' I can still remember having that discussion. We just differed a little bit on our philosophy."[1]

"You haven't taught until they have learned."

It's a simple statement with a deep meaning.

The first time I heard that statement was from Coach Wooden. As a college basketball coach who was frustrated with my players' rebounding efficiency, I telephoned him and said, "Coach, I have taught my team to rebound, but they just don't learn." I fully expected him to respond with some of his methods for improving rebounding proficiency. Instead, he said, *"Swen, you say you taught them, but you have not taught until they have learned."*

Instantly he changed my definition of "teaching." Until then, for me, teaching meant the act of passing information to students. That is why I told Coach I had "taught" my basketball players. But after that moment, the focus of teaching shifted from the teacher to the student—from giving information to learning. A new and improved question spawned, one from the perspective of the student rather than the teacher. "Coach, why have I not been able to teach my players how to rebound?" The responsibility of student learning was taken away from the student and placed on the teacher. Success became student learning and student learning alone. No matter how clever I designed my lesson, or how smoothly it went, if the students didn't learn, I had not taught.

In preparation for our next practice session, I carefully analyzed each of my taller players' abilities, limitations, and needs in respect to rebounding. I altered my teaching of rebounding, tailoring activities and strategies so that each individual would improve. For example, I worked with one of my players for a half hour before practice. During the practice, I assigned an assistant coach to another player who needed constant reminders to rebound. The coach yelled, "Go after the ball!" each time a shot was taken. During practices, I began to take notes on the improvements and needs of each player and in doing so, took notes on my own teaching. I had "learned" that good teaching includes focusing on student learning rather than pedagogical methods and strategies. I learned to focus on how each student learns. It was quite a change for me.

Once again, the philosophy and practice of Coach Wooden accords what many researchers now regard as the key to effective teaching—a laser-like focus on what students are learning or not learning.[2] When a teacher's attention strays to other matters, problems can arise. One of the most serious is an ends-means reversal. Visiting a middle school once, Gallimore was invited to observe the innovative social studies program that had been implemented two years earlier. The school leadership and the faculty were enthusiastic about the progress they had made. A key to the program was cooperative learning groups. A teacher reported that it took the team many months to stabilize the groups and get the kind of student collaborations they wanted. Achieving this had been more difficult than anticipated. But now everyone at the school was delighted with how well the groups were working. When asked about the results of the effort, essentially the same report was repeated. The cooperative groups were working great, but it was clear that the team had lost sight of the ends of their new program—improved student learning. Instead, they had been so focused on the means (cooperative groups) that they began to regard it as the end. They thought that because they were using cooperative group instruction so well, the students were surely learning. When they looked closer, to their astonishment, the students had not really benefited much from all of the effort that went into the cooperative groups project. When asked by a visiting researcher about the cooperative groups, one student said, "They're OK, but they keep us from getting our work done."

Courtesy of Indiana State University
Indiana State University players huddle around Coach Wooden to listen to his instruction. He believes a teacher has not taught until the students have learned.

Improving students' learning is the point, not simply changing teaching so it "looks" innovative or matches some instructional ideal. Whenever some "new" kind of teaching is tried, the point is that students learn more. The moment the focus shifts from what students are learning is the moment teachers risk getting off track. The end is student learning; the means is teaching. One does not become a better teacher just by adopting an approach that is in fashion or recommended. Teachers are more effective when their students learn more.

When Coach Wooden's teaching methods are analyzed, a recommended or name-brand system of teaching isn't found. As the previous chapters have attempted to illustrate, what is found is a variety of time- and practice-tested methods, many of which were identified or developed because one of his students was not learning, and he took the responsibility to correct that. By making that commitment, he adapted his teaching to what they needed, rather than trying to make them learn from the teaching he already knew how to do.

Coach Wooden was a special teacher because he accepted the idea embodied in the title of this chapter—*You haven't taught until they have learned.* There are other special teachers, and they all follow this same principle, adding evidence that it is something all teachers might emulate to good effect.

Favorite Teachers

Most people can remember at least one favorite teacher that made learning exciting. For me, my handful of special teachers made learning fun, had a passion for the subject, and deeply cared, but the bottom line was that they taught until I had learned, even when I was slow to learn. They found ways to get through so that I would gain the appetite, means, and motivation to absorb and digest the material. After immigrating to the US from the Netherlands and entering fourth grade one week after I arrived, Mrs. Rudgers, my fourth grade teacher, taught me how to read English from scratch. Prior to beginning her class, my English vocabulary consisted of five words. She easily could have considered the task of elevating my reading to the fourth-grade level too daunting, but she didn't.

I was one of 25 students, many of whom were high maintenance or downright recalcitrant. I was not much different. For the first three weeks of school, I managed to get into a fist-fight every day, thus perfecting the trip from the classroom and to the principal's office. But Mrs. Rudgers never gave up on me.

She noticed that I had a gift for mathematics. Perhaps my proficiency was not due to the gift, but rather to the fact I had already covered the material in the third grade in Holland. What the rest of the students were attempting to learn in the class was review for me. My teacher took advantage of it and found a way, during half of the math hour, to engage the rest of the students so she could take me aside for reading instruction.

Mrs. Rudgers' first lesson began in front of a photograph hanging on the classroom wall. It was a picture of a sailing ship. She pointed at the picture and said, "Picture." Carefully trying to figure out what she was trying to communicate I responded, "Boat." Boat is one of the few words found in both English and my native Dutch. Quickly and excitedly, she said, "Yes, yes, boat," pointing at the boat in the picture. "But," she said, running her hands around the frame, "picture, picture." And those were the first two English words I learned in America. Mrs. Rudgers wrote down the word for me and I never forgot it. She eventually taught me hundreds of words and introduced me to "Dick and Jane."

It must have been difficult for my teacher. There were many days when I seemed to learn nothing or even regress, forgetting past lessons and words. But she never gave up. Her persistence paid off. By the end of fourth grade I was reading at a fifth-grade level, surpassing many of my classmates.

In the early 1960s, Coach Wooden had a similar challenge, albeit not as tough a case as Mrs. Rudgers had. Keith Erickson, a very talented UCLA forward, was assigned the most important position in the UCLA full-court press—the last line of defense. Besides being a clear and skilled communicator to the players in front of him, the primary responsibilities of this position were to intercept long passes and, if the long pass was completed successfully, defend the opponents' numerical advantage (i.e., the two-on-one) until help arrived. A most important cognitive attribute was quick and accurate discernment about whether or not to gamble in an attempt to intercept a long pass. Good judgment led to a steal, but an error often led to a quick score by the opponent. A skilled back defender, who had proven his keen perspicacity, gained the trust of his teammates in front of him and gave them the confidence to become aggressive in application of the full-court press. In other words, he was able to cover their errors.

Although Erickson was very talented, he required extra practice, especially in the area of judgment. The time allotted for individual attention during the course of a practice session was insufficient for Coach to help Erickson learn to the degree of excellence necessary. But it was imperative that Erickson learn, so Coach Wooden worked with him before practice. At first the individual sessions were every day, as Wooden devised tailor-made drills. Later, the sessions occurred two or three times per week.

In order to make the right decision about intercepting the long pass, Coach taught Erickson to watch the inbound passer's hind foot. If it dropped back, he was probably telegraphing the long pass down the court into Erickson's area. Although assertiveness was a trait Erickson possessed, he had to learn to make the "educated" gamble. In the earlier sessions, he made many wrong choices, but improved daily. Erickson's competitive spirit and quickness, coupled with Coach Wooden's innovative teaching, helped make him the best back defender UCLA ever had. He became a key player in the first two national championships, largely a result of the feared UCLA full-court press in which Erickson played so vital a role.

What Special Teachers Have in Common

In an informal survey, a number of students and teachers were asked to remember a special teacher they had and to list the qualities that made those teachers special. The survey's participants formed a diverse group, which included adults in education, research, and business communities, and students in public schools, some who were receiving remedial tutoring.

John Wooden's intense passion for the game of basketball carried over from his playing days at Purdue University to his legendary coaching career.

The term "favorite" was used for increased objectivity. The intent was to encourage a wide range of nominations and descriptions, including teachers that were "easy" and let students get away with less than their best. But no one nominated such a teacher. From the descriptions received, 11 common practices of good teaching were extracted, all directly related to challenge and engagement. Coach Wooden practiced all 11, which are described in detail below.

1. They make learning engaging

Even the most seemingly uninteresting or demanding material can be made engaging in the hands of teachers who believe that making learning enjoyable is essential. UCLA basketball practices were always fun, primarily because they included a good balance of drill and playing competitive basketball. Coach Wooden, knowing the practical value of competition for learning and maintaining interest, balanced the drill-to-competition ratio. Drills taught and reinforced the basic fundamentals of the game, such as dribbling, passing, shooting, and rebounding. One drill, the "three-on-two conditioner," (which was a lot of fun, by the way) focused on conditioning, but the rest of practice was devoted to breaking down our offense and defense into one-on-one, two-on-two, three-on-three, four-on-four, and five-on-five situations. These "breakdown" activities were always competitive, and my teammates and I always looked forward to them.

"I believe in preparing my players to play the game. Fundamentals and conditioning are important toward that end, but, since I'm preparing them to play, I must have them play, compete, and test the things being presented. In other words, I must put them in competition so I can see if I have taught them."[3]

2. They have a passion for the material

Teachers with passions for their subject matter have minds that overflow with exciting information. Their souls burn with a desire to witness the students' joy of discovery. A recent Jeopardy® champion, a high school history teacher, claimed that his students thought of him as eccentric because when he was about to teach something he was excited about, he performed a little shuffle in the front of the classroom. Coach Wooden's literature teacher had a passion for Hamlet and Macbeth and a strong desire to share with his students his intimate and deep knowledge of these texts. For such teachers, teaching is not formal instruction; teaching is shared passion. And Coach Wooden's passion for teaching basketball was no different.

Most of his players had learned of their coach's success as a player. In fact, Coach was nothing short of legendary. During his senior year at Purdue University in 1932, when he was named an All-American for the third consecutive year, many considered him the best basketball player in the world, which included the professional ranks. It was said that when he drove to the hoop, defenders either got out of the way or they got hurt. It was also said that he reveled in guarding the best player on the other team because he loved a tough challenge. Legend has it that he never tired and played almost every minute of every game. His college coach, Ward Lambert, said Coach Wooden was the best-conditioned athlete he had ever seen. But above all, his passion as a player was for the beauty and effectiveness of team basketball. When he became a coach, the passion did not change.

So, if the curriculum Coach Wooden was teaching on the basketball court had a title, it would have been something like, "Developing Skilled and Powerful Individual Play for the Purpose of Using Every Move for the Benefit of Team Improvement."

Newcomers to the UCLA system, usually revered as high-scoring stars on their previous teams, were surprised Coach never condoned individual, flashy moves. On the court and in the media, Coach Wooden never gave credit to the scorers. Rather, he made concerted efforts to provide recognition to those who did the little, unheralded things that helped make the Bruins a great "team," things such as passing, setting screens, and defending. Those were the things he became genuinely excited about. In time, the newcomers began to understand this and take on a similar mindset. The motto of UCLA teams, due to their leader's passion for the sacrifice of self for the group, became one of the Coach's maxims: *"It's amazing what a team can accomplish when no one cares who receives the credit."*[4]

3. They have deep subject knowledge

Passion often leads to digging deeper into the subject, looking for more and more knowledge. And each level poses questions the answers to which are only available in a deeper level of study.

Teachers who have passions for the subjects they teach have often taken them up as hobbies. Unquenched curiosity leads them to reading and research beyond school hours, enabling them to develop deeper subject knowledge. In addition to his love of good books, basketball was Coach Wooden's hobby. At UCLA, he spent his off-seasons researching the components of basketball one subject at a time. For example, one entire spring and summer was dedicated to studying the fast break.

The accumulation of Coach Wooden's basketball knowledge led to an understanding far deeper than many coaches who opposed him. For example, he believed the little things (e.g., preventing a blister) could make the difference between winning a title and coming in second. Therefore, he placed significant and sustained emphasis on making certain his players practiced the correct method of putting their socks on and lacing their shoes.

4. They are extremely organized

Favorite teachers were organized. Through creating school-year goals and lesson plans to accomplish those objectives, they were able to keep students on track. Staying on track kept students cognizant of the relevancy of each lesson.

In other words, lessons were sequenced for the accomplishment of a specific goal. Students commented that, as a result, interest and motivation were sparked and maintained.

It may be easier for basketball students, rather than classroom students, to figure out how a practice activity fits in the overall purpose of a practice session. Nevertheless, Coach Wooden's organization demonstrated the accumulative nature of drill sequencing, the necessity of each component, and the clear relativity of every activity to the goal of the team. At no moment in a practice session were we doubtful of an activity's value. My teammates and I were continuously learning "parts" and putting them together until we had something complete, like an offensive play or defensive stunt.

5. They are intense

Favorite teachers were skilled at maintaining learning intensity for long durations of classroom time. When asked how, surprisingly most survey respondents did not say anything about the teacher becoming overly animated in order to keep students' interest. Rather, teacher success seemed to be related to organization, teacher passion, deep knowledge, and enthusiasm, things which continue to spark student interest.

Again, pulling this off on the court is easier than in a classroom. Maintaining intensity in a high school physical education class, for example, can't be compared to the challenges of a history class. But in either case, a slow pace and a lull in the action can result in distraction and loss of focus.

Coach Wooden was able to build and maintain the intensity for an entire two-and-one-half hour practice session. But he never worked at it, or used "tricks." We wanted to learn. We wanted to keep putting parts together into larger combinations to see if they worked. We continued our focus even when we messed up a little, and found ways to fix our mistakes. I'm certain some of us in the 21st century would have been labeled "ADD" (Attention Deficit Disorder) or "ADHD" (Attention Deficit Hyperactivity Disorder) in a classroom, but not on Coach Wooden's court.

6. They know students need to be recognized for even small progress

Not surprisingly, a qualification for being a "favorite" teacher is encouragement. These expert motivators were skilled at balancing encouragement with challenge. In other words, after severely challenging students, perhaps to the brink of discouragement, just in time, when the students did something right, the teachers acknowledged it and, thereby, brought the students' back to a place where they didn't give up and were able to be challenged again. In addition, they never gave up on a student.

For several months, Tharp and Gallimore recorded everything Coach Wooden said during dozens of practice sessions.[5] After analyzing the data, they were surprised, among other things, to learn that his encouraging comments directed to players were few and far between. However, because he was so keenly observant of the individual players and their needs, he usually delivered encouragement when encouragement was needed. The players had to work hard for his praise, probably because he wanted intrinsic motivation and was loath to encourage them to work for his approval as opposed to self-satisfaction. But he did let his players know when progress was made, always immediately after they did something correct, and when he did, he was explicit about what they had accomplished. He didn't just say "good," he said what the good thing was.

7. They treat everyone with respect

There is an old adage that states, "To get respect, give it." One way Coach exhibited this was described in Chapter 1 in his treatment of janitors who cared for the visiting locker rooms; he always made sure his teams left them clean before they departed. A way he showed respect for his students was to openly say that while he might not like everyone, he loved everyone, and that he understood that not everyone would like him. But he hoped they would not let that possibility stand in the way of a productive teaching-learning relationship. In the way he treated his players, most of us came to understand that he meant it when he said he loved each one of us in the sense that he deeply cared that each one got a good education and learned to be a better basketball player.

8. They are fair

This may be the most difficult for a teacher to pull off, but every survey respondent included it. They all said their favorite teachers were fair.

For Coach Wooden, fairness was giving each student the treatment he earned or deserved. Oddly, that meant all students were treated differently. At first glance, many perceive "different treatment" as unfair. And although he was confident what he was doing was fair, the possibility that his players didn't understand concerned Coach then and it concerns him to this day. *"I hope I was fair to all my players,"* he has said on many occasions. In time, most of his players understood that he was fair.

9. They believe all students are natural learners

Seeing beyond the "attitudes" and "outward dispositions" of resistant children, these teachers saw all children as young adults who truly wanted to learn. Why not? Teachers know, from the moment children are born, they are ravenous and incessant learners with insatiable appetites for discovering the world around them. Why should that hunger stop when they enter the school years? It doesn't. Favorite teachers know that and assume every child wants to

Courtesy of UT Lady Vols Media Relations

University of Tennessee women's basketball coach Pat Summitt, who had Coach Wooden speak to her team in 2002, has been called the John Wooden of women's basketball.

learn. They believe learning comes naturally for children, although teachers may have to try different ways to make that happen.

As a novice basketball player my first year at UCLA, I made more errors than any other player. Obtuse and downright "dingy" at times, I'm certain I tested Coach Wooden's patience. As I look back on that experience, I'm frankly surprised he didn't give up on me. I received many reproofs, but through it all, he never gave up. He believed I was capable of learning just like the rest of the players. I'm thankful he believed in me. It has made all the difference in my life.

10. They make it implicitly known they like being with their students

These teachers not only made class fun, they also radiated with an unsaid statement that clearly communicated to students, "I like being with you. You give me enjoyment."

In the three years I attended UCLA, Coach Wooden made a conscious effort to personally greet me when I arrived at practice and at games. He usually asked personal questions before getting into basketball. Then, he turned to helping individual players with personal basketball needs. He was out on the practice floor running shooting drills, defensive drills, rebounding drills, etc. He loved it. He was like a fish in water when he taught us.

But beyond the game and the fundamentals, drills, playing, and competing, he loved being with us. He always considered us his "boys." *"Next to family, you are my family,"* he said often. We also loved being with him.

11. They place priority on individualized teaching

Classroom teachers don't teach classrooms, they teach individuals. Basketball coaches don't teach teams, they teach players. The merging of players' skills makes up a team. The emphasis on the development of individuals, and the ability to blend talents into a smooth-working unit, may have been Coach Wooden's greatest strength.

When teaching the UCLA high-post offense, for example, there was nothing general about his teaching methods. He did not compliment or critique the team's performance nearly as often as addressing individuals about specific teaching points.

"Bill, not like that. Do it like this."

"Keith, make the reverse pivot."

"Larry, this is the time to go for the offensive rebound. You were too late."

The consistent constructive attention to the players helped each of us understand how important we were to him and therefore, to the team.

These 11 qualities of favorite teachers are true of teachers whose students learn. But excellence cannot be reached by working on these qualities. It seems there is a "prerequisite causer." That "causer" is most clearly an uncompromising commitment that all individuals assimilate the curriculum requirements. Anyone who has taken on the title of "teacher" has accepted the responsibility to instruct, and therefore has eliminated easy use of excuses for "children of difficulty." Many teachers say teaching is much more than a job, and it certainly is. Teaching is accountability, a responsibility to each individual under the teacher's supervision. Therefore, the 11 qualities of effective teachers are not the ends. They are the means, naturally resulting from the creative and innovative teachers who begin with an immutable conviction that each student learns, and who will stop at nothing to devise whatever means are necessary for each student to learn.

This understanding directed the moves Coach Wooden made as a teacher. He learned and employed the essential ingredients of effective teaching as a result of his commitment that each student is to meet or surpass the requirements—the required curriculum of the English course or his own basketball curriculum—created to develop skilled individuals whose collection of talents formed a championship team.

"I believe teaching is all about students learning. When I taught high school English, I had a variety of students in each of my six daily classes. Shortly after

I began teaching, I became convinced that students are so different from each other in so many ways. Some came from the country club area while others lived on the other side of the tracks. Some may have had a more difficult time learning certain subjects while others were somewhat gifted. Because of those differences and also because of my commitment to help each one of them reach their potential, I began employing different teaching strategies for them. But I did not sit down and simply design strategies or attend seminars about methods and employ them. Those who presented the seminars did not know my children. I knew them and I designed methods and strategies to fit their particular needs.

"I also learned, in order to help children learn, they must become interested in the subject I was teaching. I was fortunate to have attended the classrooms of some very good instructors and professors during my elementary, middle, high school, undergraduate, and graduate years. Mrs. Henley made me want to come to class. Dr. Kriek made me eager to learn. I found myself counting the hours until his next class. His way of teaching was so interesting it made me wonder what he was going to do next. Dr. Sears, American History, caused none of us to want to miss even one day of class. Dr. Ladell, who taught Shakespeare, would always make a statement, or ask a question, to get you thinking. He gave us a hint about something that made us want to find out more. He may have mentioned something about a character and you found yourself in the library looking him or her up.

"And there were others who simply threw the material at us and expected us to learn that way. Generally, their reasons for that style, especially the college professors, was they believed college students don't need their interest generated. They said students should be interested because they are in college to graduate. I don't agree. Students of all ages learn better when interest is generated.

"I truly believe these wonderful teachers I have mentioned all loved the subjects they taught. I have been asked, in order to become a great teacher, if it's important to know your subject deeply. Of course it is. The deeper you know the subject, the more you are likely to fall in love with it, and the more likely you are to continue to dig deeper and deeper. That enthusiasm is contagious for students. Dr. Ladell, for example, had to know Hamlet deeply in order to ask those questions which started our wheels turning and our appetites growling. He already knew the answers.

"For those teachers I have mentioned, and also for me, teaching is much more than a job. It is a responsibility to those under my supervision—a responsibility to teach them. And how can I tell if I've taught them, if I've been successful? Right. Only if they've learned. Therefore, I have learned to focus on studying people, especially young people. I study the way they react, *the way they are motivated, the way they are frustrated, and the way they work. This will help me discover the way they learn and when I discover that, I'm half way there. The methods I learned, both for the classroom and for the court, were created from and for my students."*[6]

Conclusion

Dwight Chapin's biography of Coach Wooden's success was titled *The Wizard of Westwood*, which is a term many have used as a moniker for Coach. But if anyone mentions the nickname to him, he will say, *"I don't like it. I'm no wizard. I'm a teacher."*[7] He believes that his success came not from wizardry but from the steady application of a teaching philosophy and practice based on the idea that *"you haven't taught until they have learned."*

"Profound responsibilities come with teaching and coaching. You can do so much good—or harm. It's why I believe that next to parenting, teaching and coaching are the two most important professions in the world."

John Wooden[1]

Chapter 8

It's What the Teachers are Themselves

Ask Coach Wooden what is the most important idea teachers need to know, and he says, *"Way back in the mid-'30s I picked up something and I never forgot it: No written word, no spoken plea can teach our youth what they should be. Nor all the books on all the shelves, it's what the teachers are themselves."*
— anonymous author[2]

Coach Wooden believes there are many things the dedicated teacher has to do. Each of the previous seven chapters has presented some of the principles and practices he believes apply to all teaching. Establish a teaching-learning relationship with students, and get to know them so well that you can provide the exact instruction that each student needs. Teach your students to be motivated by success defined as peace of mind that comes from doing the best they can, and not to worry about how they compare to others. Learn as much about your subject matter as possible to deeply understand it, and throughout your career keep learning all that you can. Keep notes, analyze your lessons, and focus on what did and did not help students learn. Plan and plan some more, Coach Wooden would say, so you can perfect tomorrow's lessons. Master the arts of pedagogy, and when students struggle, look first to what you can do to help them learn, instead of blaming them, their parents, the school administrators, or society.

Yes, all of those things, Coach Wooden believes, are critical to good teaching, but he would say the most important of all is this: *"It's what the teachers are themselves."* It's the first thing he says if you ask him to talk about teaching. And then he adds, *"I always tried to teach by example."*[3]

Courtesy of Mitch Gordon

Not a day goes by that Coach Wooden doesn't hear from a former player expressing his gratitude for the example his coach set by living a life true to his teachings.

Do the examples teachers set achieve their intended outcome? Teachers may know how well students did in their class this year. Perhaps they will know how well they did a few years later. But Coach Wooden believes, *"You won't know what kind of teacher you were until 20 years after the fact."*[4]

He first heard this as a young teacher, but for him its truth was only fully validated long after his last year of teaching basketball. Toward the end of his career and even more often after his retirement from teaching and coaching, increasing numbers of former students and players began returning, sometimes after years of little or no contact, saying, "Now that I'm a teacher, leader, parent, and/or coach, I have found myself following the example you set for us and it's made a difference in my life."

Those who join this appreciation chorus focus more on who Coach Wooden was than anything else. They focus on his character and the example he set, captured in his many maxims such as:

- *"Be quick but don't hurry."*
- *"Talent will get you to the top but it takes character to keep you there."*
- *"Make each day a masterpiece."*
- *"I can build your conditioning through practice sessions but you can tear it down between practices if you don't take care of yourself."*
- *"It's amazing what a team can accomplish when no one cares who receives the credit."*
- *"Make friendship a fine art."*
- *"You are no better than anyone else and no one is better than you."*
- *"Have character; don't be one."*
- *"Be more concerned with your character than your reputation; your character is what you really are while your reputation is merely what others think you are."*[5]

But it was not the maxims that influenced us so much; it was that our teacher practiced them. Coach Wooden was quick but never hurried. His character kept him in first place. He strove to make each day a masterpiece. He took care of himself between practices. He never accepted credit not due him. He worked hard at developing friendships. He never accepted the position of celebrity. And he understood the preeminence of character over reputation and was concerned solely with the former. At one time or another, every one of his students and players heard him recite the poem that introduced this chapter and which captures his understanding of the importance of a teacher's example.

> No written word, no spoken plea can teach our youth what they should be.
> Nor all the books on all the shelves, it's what the teachers are themselves.
> — anonymous author

What a challenge! For some, being a role model may be a moderate challenge and for others, it might require a complete makeover. Whatever the case, if you are up to the challenge, the first step is understanding that teaching is a moral profession.

Teaching is a Moral Profession

When Coach Wooden says *"what teachers are themselves"* and *"teaching by example,"* he is thinking of teaching as a moral profession.[6] It is a profession because it has specialized activities, the practices of teaching. It is moral because its purpose is serving the best interests of the students and not the teacher's self-interest. Its purpose is not personal wealth, acknowledgment, or social status, although almost all teachers would be happy to have a bit more of each.

To practice a moral profession requires a set of orienting values and ethics—among others, a steady sense of fairness and justice, truthfulness, and commitment to principle over expediency. Without orienting values and ethics, a teacher is at sea without a moral anchor. How the teacher responds, perhaps in the midst of a torrent of angry words, counter-claims, and threats depends on a personal moral compass, the clarity of personally held values and ethical principles.

Experience counts a lot. The veterans who have the experience and moral grounding are quickly identified by the novices as indispensable sources of advice. No doubt experience plays a role in developing teachers' professional judgment, but that alone is not sufficient. No matter how long one teaches, challenges arise for which experience alone is no preparation. These cannot be dealt with by recipe and formula. There is no handy rulebook to refer to when they arise—on the first day of a career and on the last. The challenges can be dealt with only if a teacher has an ethical and moral grounding.

This is the meaning of Coach Wooden's commitment to teach by example. Whatever students learn in a classroom, one thing they certainly learn is how their teachers behave in the face of ethical and moral challenges. *"It's what the teachers are themselves."*

Teaching Requires Courage

A moral and ethical foundation is necessary, but not sufficient. Teachers must also have courage.

Courage of Convictions. The courage of convictions means standing firm when inappropriate, illegitimate, or threatening demands are made. It means having the courage needed to uphold academic and social standards when there is pressure to relax them or make exceptions in individual cases.

Every day, teachers confront challenges to their convictions. The challenges come in many forms. One student accuses another of stealing, cheating, or bullying, and turns to the teacher for resolution, restitution, and simple justice. A student misses a high-stakes deadline, and offers an excuse. Coach Wooden was not immune to these problems. Once, the father of one of his high school players threatened to get him fired. The player had been benched for breaking a team rule. Despite the threat from the father, Coach stood his ground. It was strongly held values and principles that gave him the courage to stand firm.

Small day-to-day challenges are the most immediate and frequent kind. But there are more challenging ones. For example, dealing with students whose performances do not match their aspirations. If it is clear that students can do the work, or reach their goals, then pleasant or not, it is the teacher's obligation to provide unvarnished feedback. "If you want to reach your goals, you will need to do better. Here's what you need to do, and here's how I can help you, IF you are willing to put in the effort."

Coach Wooden believes in team play. He expected even his most gifted athletes to play within a team framework. On more than one occasion, he resisted efforts by exceptional players to introduce what Coach referred to as "fancy stuff," or individual play. His insistence on this standard was so strong that he would play a less talented but team-oriented player over someone with more individual star potential. Sometimes star players confronted him. Some even threatened to quit. In one case, he anticipated a player leaving, so he called the parents to alert them to their son's unhappiness and to explain what he saw was happening. The player did not leave, and went on to buy into Coach Wooden's philosophy, play for UCLA, and help lead the Bruins to two national championships—all as a team player.

But what if a student continues to resist a teacher's standards and feedback? What if a student (and perhaps a parent) pressures a teacher to accept a substandard science report? What if a student facing failure to graduate to the next grade has not done the required work, and refuses? What if a star student with a brilliant future is discovered to have submitted a plagiarized paper in the last month of his or her senior year of high school? Each of these challenges takes the courage of conviction to effectively confront the individual in a way that aids and does not injure, that teaches and not just punishes.

Courage to Self-Examine. To develop their full capacity, teachers must honestly, objectively examine their practice, identify shortcomings, accept criticism, and work for self-improvement. If teachers do not have the courage to self-examine, they cannot set an example for their students. Making errors and mistakes are a shortcoming only if one does not learn from them. How many times have students heard that piece of advice? But that advice also applies to teachers, who must have the courage to practice what they preach.

The need to self-examine is increasing. Teachers are being asked to learn new ways of teaching so that their students are able to meet new and more challenging standards. This requires major changes in instructional practice. To learn those new methods, teachers will need to look at themselves in self-critical ways. Increasingly, they are turning to colleagues to be collaborators, *critical friends* who will help each other learn new approaches. It means finding opportunities to observe and analyze alternative teaching forms, and to try them out, struggle, and find a way to change their own practices. This takes courage, just as in any profession that depends on reflection and analysis of practice as the basis for making improvements.

Consider the following example.[7] Twenty-eight teachers from seven countries, including Australia, Czech Republic, Hong Kong, Japan, the Netherlands, Switzerland, and the US, were videotaped by a research team. These 28 teachers agreed to release tapes of lessons they taught, so that others could learn about different methods of mathematics teaching. The 28 lessons were selected because they were typical lessons in each of the seven countries. None of the lessons were chosen because they were exemplary, so the teachers were not always showing their best work—just the way they taught every day in the classroom.

One of the teachers who agreed to release lesson tapes was Crystal Lancour. In 2003, Lancour attended a conference of mathematics teachers. One of the conference activities was viewing and discussing some of the 28 videos that had been released for public use. At first, some conference attendees doubted the value of intensely studying a few videos of ordinary mathematics lessons. Why not spend the time analyzing exemplary lessons, many asked? But as the day wore on, more and more of the conference attendees became excited about what they could learn by collaboratively watching and analyzing typical math lessons.

During a break, the conference participants were informed that in the audience was one of the U.S. teachers who had released her lessons for public viewing. There was an audible gasp followed by immediate and spontaneous applause. A second round of even louder applause greeted Lancour as she was introduced and rose to be identified. They were not applauding the lesson that she had taught—because they had not yet seen it. They were applauding her courage for having released one of her ordinary, everyday lessons so that others might study and learn from it.

The example Lancour set is one to admire. It takes courage for teachers to look critically at their classroom practices in order to improve their teaching. It takes even more courage to be observed and to receive feedback on how to improve. Whether researching their own teaching to improve it, exposing the gaps in their subject matter knowledge, or being observed and videotaped, courage is needed. It's never easy to risk exposing possible shortcomings. No one is completely comfortable with professional criticism or commentary, no matter how kindly it is offered. But sometimes that's the only way to discover what one needs to learn and change. If you choose to teach, you risk a certain amount of exposure to advice and criticism, often from students if not from fellow professionals. Veteran teachers will surely agree.

Although he is viewed today as a positive role model and cultural icon, Coach Wooden is the first to say he made mistakes, that he kept learning throughout his long teaching career. *"I'm human. We all are. We all make mistakes."*[8]

The critical test is whether we have the courage to examine ourselves, and try to learn from those mistakes. Even today, in the 10th decade of his life, Coach Wooden reflects on his teaching career to ponder judgments and deeds that he might do differently, with the wisdom of hindsight.

"Looking back, I think I sometimes failed to get reserves to feel how important they were. Over time, some of my players began to tell me that. My intentions were to make the reserves feel important to the team, and I thought I did. I guess I was fooling myself."[9]

He authorized a biography that included lengthy comments by former players, some critical of coaching decisions.[10] That he authorized a biography that included the critical comments is a testament to his courage and commitment to examining his practice.

In his own autobiography, he provided more reflections on things he wished he had done differently.[11] For example, he recounts the time he kicked one of his best high school players off the team for violating a strict no smoking rule during the season. At the time, Coach Wooden writes, the young man was on his way to an athletic scholarship and a college education. Once dismissed from the team, the boy dropped out of high school without graduating and lived a life of low-paying jobs. Looking back more than 65 years later, Coach believes he made a mistake. From this instance and many others, he learned to deal with such situations very differently. One of his maxims is *"when you are through learning, you are through."* He taught it, and he lived it.

Courage of Commitment. A final challenge that takes courage is the context in which many teachers work. Low pay, poor working conditions, dilapidated facilities, and a lack of support are a few of the most common. To remain com-

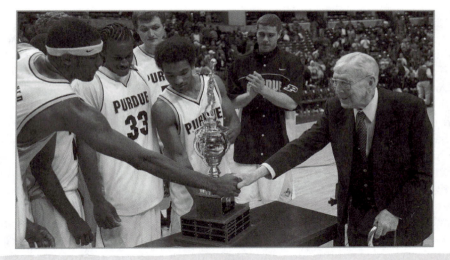

Through the Wooden Tradition in Indianapolis, Indiana, and the Wooden Classic in Anaheim, California, Coach Wooden is still able to impact the lives of college basketball players.

mitted to students, and to all the things outlined in this book, takes an extraordinary degree of courage.

When Coach Wooden accepted the position of UCLA head basketball coach he was told that very soon a new basketball facility would be constructed. But for more than 15 years, his teams either played home games in a small gym on campus, or on borrowed courts in the area. Many other promises were not kept for some time. Although he was not happy about the working conditions, and the many disadvantages his teams confronted without a proper home court, he remained steadfast. In time, some promises were fulfilled and some were not.

"Maybe the most amazing fact of all those associated with the John Wooden Era is the salary he made in his final year as UCLA coach. It was $32,500. No, there are no zeroes missing! That's the actual number .... Actually, the story gets worse. When Wooden originally accepted the job for the princely sum of $6,000 in 1948, he didn't know that his checks were being signed by the president of the student association. The Associated Students weren't paying into a retirement fund, so as a result, Wooden earned no retirement benefits from his first twelve years on the job .... In the midst of all of UCLA's glowing basketball success, the Wooden salary issue remains a lingering disgrace."[12]

Despite the unfulfilled promises and seeming lack of support for what he had accomplished, for 47 years Coach Wooden taught his lessons and perfected his teaching philosophy and practice. He had that peace of mind that comes only from doing the best of which you are capable.

In too many communities throughout the nation, teachers work in situations that try their patience and dim their hopes. Hungry children, overcrowded classes, inadequate books, largely useless professional development, impossible demands, hostile media, and changing policies are just a few of the challenges presented. Even in well-run, well-equipped, and professionally administered schools, discouragement and disappointment can become constant companions.

To work through these conditions and find a way to persevere, teachers must sustain the "optimism that is true moral courage," to borrow a maxim credited to Ernest Shackleton.[13] This is why teaching is the greatest act of optimism.[14] It is an optimism that one's efforts can matter for students, that personal effort, dedication, and commitment to teaching might have some effect, whether great or small.

A Little Fellow Follows Me

A careful man I want to be.
A little man follows me.
I do not dare go astray,
For fear he'll go the self same way.

I cannot once escape his eyes.
Whate'er he sees me do he tries.
Like me he says he's going to be,
The little fellow who follows me.

He thinks that I am good and fine.
Believe in every word of mine.
The base in me he must not see,
The little man that follows me.

I must remember as I go
Through summer's sun and winter's snow,
I am building for the years that be,
For that little chap who follows me.

Lee Fisher

Nowhere is that optimism more clearly seen than in a poem Coach Wooden often quotes when discussing teaching. When he reads it, he reads it with conviction of its words and in the hope that he lived up to the challenge.

At the beginning of this chapter, Coach Wooden is quoted as saying, *"You won't know what kind of teacher you were until 20 years after the fact."* For Coach, it has been 20 years and counting. Not a day goes by that he doesn't receive a phone call or visit from at least one of his former students. The jury is in on what kind of role model John Wooden was and whether or not he taught his students "what they should be." In his authorized biography, many former players testified to the impact his example had in their lives.[15]

"Coach Wooden was my high school coach. For two years I was his assistant at Indiana State, and when he went to UCLA I went with him .... I had him as an English teacher in high school. He was a good teacher .... Sometimes I think of John as a father figure, a brother, a coach, but always a friend."
— Ed Powell, student of and assistant to Coach Wooden

"I came out of a rather disturbed home life .... Whatever good values and standards of ethics that I might have today I attribute to my association with John Wooden, and looking at his values and learning from him, the standards he set, the character he acted out. What he not only spoke about, but acted and lived, has held me in very good stead."
— Stan Jacobs, student manager of high school and college teams coached by Coach Wooden

"I played for Wooden in 1937 and 1938 .... He had a tremendous effect on me .... [Once we drove down to southern Indiana] and stopped at Logansport. We were supposed to have a meal there. Pete Donaldson, a black man on our team, sat down, but they went to Coach and told him [Pete] had to eat in the kitchen. That's fifty years ago. And [Coach] says, 'Let's go somewhere else.' And we did."
— Sebastian Nowicki, coached by Coach Wooden in high school

"It's hard to put into words all the different ways Coach Wooden has had an impact on me. He is a shining example of what you can do if you keep yourself in shape and treat everyone well around you—good things will happen."
— Lucius Allen, coached by Coach Wooden at UCLA

"I learned from his extraordinarily detailed organization. He was fantastically prepared, literally every practice was planned down to the minute. You don't lose track of lessons like that. When you are preparing for a major busi-

ness presentation fifteen years later, you look around and you're probably the best prepared person there. Well, why is that true? Because people like [Coach Wooden] proved to you at an early stage of development that the time spent in preparation will pay off."
— Pete Blackman, coached by Coach Wooden at UCLA

"UCLA is a really tough place to play basketball and that makes what John Wooden did even more amazing when you consider all the people he had to keep happy—if not happy, at least satisfied, and if not satisfied, at least still on the team or in the school .... What I learned from John Wooden about life is the basic faith that things in the long run will work out. If you have principles, stick to them even if they cost you some in the short run. They will help you in the long run and it will be for the best."
— Lynn Schackelford, coached by Coach Wooden at UCLA

"When I was playing for Coach Wooden, the influence wasn't as strong as now. I learned more after leaving UCLA just by judging the events in my life and comparing them to the examples he set. He set an incredible example and you don't really realize exactly what he was doing until quite some time later .... Wooden was a constant teacher and role model. I really appreciate his morality and what he was able to impart as far as how to live your life, how to enjoy success, and not let fame destroy you. I got that first hand. Success destroys a lot of people. Fame and glory and money came with the success. It never had a chance with him. That to me says a lot."
— Kareem Abdul-Jabbar, coached by Coach Wooden at UCLA

"Were we to do it over, now we would make every effort to gain the perspective of players, of assistant coaches, of Coach Wooden himself [to complement the systematic observations made during practices]. So if we could coach those two young researchers of 1974-75, those are the two points we'd put on 3 x 5 cards. Beforehand, we'd work to get the instructions phrased more tersely. We might even show them some demonstrations of how to do it better.[16] We'd give them a hustle or two: 'Goodness Gracious, call the Coach!' 'You'll never score if you don't push!' But we wouldn't give them a scolding, nor even a reproof. The data they collected are still interesting, nearly 30 years later. Neither would we praise them. They don't need it; they got that reward from others, and especially from the privilege of watching a master at the peak of his craft. His teaching changed the way they thought about all teaching. We know they'll never again see his like."
— Gallimore & Tharp, researched Coach Wooden's teaching from 1974 to present[17]

Courtesy of Mitch Gordon

Swen Nater and Ronald Gallimore, the authors of this book, both believe Coach Wooden has had a positive impact on their lives.

"It was his life that changed my life."
— Swen Nater, coached by Coach Wooden at UCLA

Coach Wooden's passion for teaching his players, children, grandchildren, and anyone else in his life is evident to nearly everyone who knows him. "'Life to him is a one-room schoolhouse,' wrote sports columnist Jim Murray. 'A pedagogue is all he ever wanted to be.' But Coach Wooden's best teaching technique is hard to pass along. Not every teacher can use the model of his own life to inspire students beyond their talents."[18]

To grasp the meaning John Wooden sees in the poem at the start of this chapter that he so often recites, and from which the title and theme of this chapter were taken, Gallimore and I asked him to comment on each phrase. What he said, we offer as the last words on his teaching principles and practices.

No written word,   *Books are wonderful sources for information, enjoyable stories, historical lessons, and moral guidance. But books are inadequate for leading children into successful adulthood. We cannot rely solely on books for the development of character.*

no spoken plea,

As eloquent and powerful as it is, The Declaration of Independence did not cause Americans to pursue values expressed in the document. Speeches, axioms, and clever sayings only spark interest in truth and, at best, gets listeners off their seats, ready for action. But spoken words, no matter how loud or how powerful, do not cause the audience to follow the speaker.

can teach our youth what they should be.

Looking upon their students, teachers often envision them in the future. Some will be doctors, some lawyers, some teachers, some farmers. But, more importantly, they see men and women who are prepared to do what is right; men and women committed to community; men and women of character. That is what youth should be.

Nor all the books all the shelves.

All the world's books, as wonderful as they are, are not on teachers of character. They may present character, but they cannot transform it from a book to the heart of a child, even if that child read every book on every shelf.

It's what the teachers are themselves.

Teachers and parents/relatives are primary role models because they are present day in and day out. Moral character can only be developed and ingrained through the moral example of parents and teachers. "Are" is a key word. Parents and teachers cannot pretend to be moral, loving, respectful, and considerate. If they really are, and not just pretending, children will follow. Only 'what the teachers are themselves' can 'teach our youth what they should be.'

Endnotes

Preface

1. J. Wooden, personal communication, March 10, 2003.
2. J. Wooden, personal communication, February 12, 2002.
3. Ibid.
4. Dickinson, R. (2003, Summer). Reminiscing and reflecting with coach John Wooden. *Indiana Basketball History Magazine, 11*(3), 8-14.
5. Wooden, J. R. (with S. Jamison). (1997). *Wooden: A lifetime of observations and reflections on and off the court*, pp. 141-142. Lincolnwood (Chicago), IL: Contemporary Books.
6. Tharp, R. G., & Gallimore, R. (1976). Basketball's John Wooden: What a coach can teach a teacher. *Psychology Today, 9*(8), 74-78.
7. Gallimore, R., & Tharp, R. (2004). What a coach can teach a teacher 1975–2004: Reflections and reanalysis of John Wooden's teaching practices. *The Sport Psychologist, 18*(2), 119-137.
8. Wooden, *Wooden: A lifetime of observations*, p. 74, emphasis original.
9. Ibid., p. 199.

Acknowledgments

1. Tharp & Gallimore, Basketball's John Wooden.
2. Gallimore & Tharp, What a coach can teach.
3. Wooden, J. R. (with S. Jamison). (2004). *My personal best: Life lessons from an All-American journey*. New York: McGraw-Hill.

Chapter One

1. J. Wooden, personal communication, February 12, 2002.
2. Tharp & Gallimore, Basketball's John Wooden; Gallimore & Tharp, What a coach can teach.
3. Gallimore & Tharp, What a coach can teach, p. 128.
4. J. Wooden, personal communication, January 4, 2005.
5. Wooden, *Wooden: A lifetime of observations*, pp. 132-134.
6. Gallimore & Tharp, What a coach can teach, p. 126.
7. Gallimore & Tharp, What a coach can teach.

8. J. Wooden, personal communication, October, 2004.

9. J. Wooden, personal communication, June, 2003.

10. Paraphrasing of "speech," approved by John Wooden, personal communication, January 4, 2005.

11. J. Wooden, personal communication, January, 2005.

12. Goldenberg, C. N. (2004). *Successful school change: Creating settings to improve teaching and learning.* New York: Teachers College Press; Tharp, R. G., Estrada, P., Dalton, S. S., & Yamauchi, L. A. (2000). *Teaching transformed: Achieving excellence, fairness, inclusion, and harmony.* Boulder, CO: Westview Press; Saunders, W., & Goldenberg, C. (2005). The contribution of settings to school improvement and school change: A case study. In C. O'Donnell & L. Yamauchi (Eds.), *Culture and context in human behavior change: Theory, research, and applications* (pp. 127-150). New York: Peter Lang; Tharp, R. G., & Gallimore, R. (1989). *Rousing minds to life: Teaching, learning, and schooling in social context.* Cambridge: Cambridge University Press.

Chapter Two

1. Johnson, N. L. (2003). *The John Wooden Pyramid of Success* (2nd ed.). Los Angeles: Cool Titles.

2. J. Wooden, personal communication, February 12, 2002.

3. Ibid.

4. Johnson, *The John Wooden Pyramid of Success,* p. 328.

5. Ibid., p. 357.

6. Ibid., p. 335.

7. Ibid., p. 303.

8. Ibid., pp. 324-325.

9. Ibid., p. 182.

10. J. Wooden, personal communication, November, 2004.

11. Stipek, D. J. (1993). *Motivation to learn.* Boston: Allyn & Bacon.

12. Ibid.

13. Stipek, *Motivation to learn;* Salmon, J. M., Givvin, K. B., Kazemi E., Saxe, G., & MacGyvers, V. L. (1998). The value (and convergence) of practices suggested by motivation research and promoted by mathematics education reformers. *Journal for Research in Mathematics Education, 29*(4), 465-488.

14. Scanlan, T. K. (2002). Social evaluation and the competition process: A developmental perspective. In F. L. Smoll & R. E. Smith (Eds.), *Children and youth in sport: A biopsychosocial perspective* (2nd ed., pp. 393-407). Dubuque, IA: Kendall/Hunt Publishing; Scanlan, T. K., Babkes, M. L., & Scanlan, L. A. (2005). Participation in sport: A devel-

opmental glimpse at emotion. In J. L. Mahoney, R. W. Larson, & J. S. Eccles, (Eds.), *Organized activities as contexts of development: Extracurricular activities, after-school and community programs* (pp. 275-309). Mahwah, NJ: Lawrence Erlbaum & Associates; Scanlan, T. K., Russell, D. G., Wilson, N. C., & Scanlan, L. A. (2003). Project on elite athlete commitment (PEAK): I. Introduction and methodology. *Journal of Sport and Exercise Psychology, 25*, 360-376.

Chapter Three

1. J. Wooden, personal communication, February 12, 2002.
2. Ibid.
3. Wooden, J. R. (1999). *Practical modern basketball* (3rd ed.). Boston: Allyn & Bacon, p. 17.
4. Ibid., p. 4.
5. J. Wooden, personal communication, 2003.
6. J. Wooden, personal communication, October, 2003.
7. J. Wooden, personal communication, February 12, 2002.
8. J. Wooden, personal communication, February, 2003.
9. J. Wooden, personal communication, October, 2003.
10. Ibid.
11. Garet, M. S., Porter, A. C., Desimone, L., Birman, B. F., & Yoon, K. S. (2001). What makes professional development effective? Results from a national sample of teachers. *American Educational Research Journal, 38*(4), 915-945.
12. Goldenberg, *Successful school change.*
13. Wooden, *Wooden: A lifetime of observations,* p. 199.
14. Crockett, M. (2002). Inquiry as professional development: Creating dilemmas through teachers' work. *Teaching and Teacher Education, 18*, 609-624.
15. Stigler, J. W., & Hiebert, J. (1999). *The teaching gap: Best ideas from the world's teachers for improving education in the classroom.* New York: Free Press.
16. Ibid., pp. 109-110.
17. Wooden, *Wooden: A lifetime of observations,* p. 143.

Chapter Four

1. National Council of Teacher Quality. Retrieved April, 2005, from http://www.nctq.org/issues/subject.html.
2. Wooden, *Practical modern basketball.*
3. Tharp & Gallimore, Basketball's John Wooden.

4. Tharp & Gallimore, Basketball's John Wooden; Gallimore & Tharp, What a coach can teach.
5. Gallimore & Tharp, What a coach can teach.
6. J. Wooden, personal communication, February, 2002.
7. Ibid.
8. J. Wooden, personal communication, 2002.
9. J. Wooden, personal communication, February, 2003.
10. J. Wooden, personal communication, October, 2003.
11. Gallimore & Tharp, What a coach can teach.
12. Shulman, L. S. (1986). Those who understand: Knowledge growth in teaching. *Educational Researcher, 15*(2), 9.
13. Hiebert, J., Morris, A. K., & Glass, B. (2003). Learning to learn to teach: An "experiment" model for teaching and teacher preparation in mathematics. *Journal of Mathematics Teacher Education, 66*, 201-222.
14. Sarason, S. (1972). *The creation of settings and the future societies.* San Francisco: Jossey-Bass, p. 123.
15. Garet et al., What makes professional development.
16. Hiebert, J., Gallimore, R., & Stigler, J. (2002). A knowledge base for the teaching profession: What would it look like, and how can we get one? *Educational Researcher, 31*(5), 3-15; Gallimore, R., & Stigler, J. (2003). Closing the teaching gap: Assisting teachers adapt to changing standards and assessments. In C. Richardson (Ed.), *Whither Assessment* (pp. 25-36). London, England: Qualifications and Curriculum Authority.
17. Stigler & Hiebert, *The teaching gap.*

Chapter Five

1. Wooden, *Wooden: A lifetime of observations*, p. viii.
2. Tharp & Gallimore, Basketball's John Wooden; Gallimore & Tharp, What a coach can teach.
3. Wooden, *Wooden: A lifetime of observations*, pp. 132-133.
4. Wooden, *Practical modern basketball*, p. 31.
5. Wooden, *Wooden: A lifetime of observations*, p. 132.
6. J. Wooden, personal communication, 2002.
7. Wooden, *Practical modern basketball*, p. 25.
8. J. Wooden, personal communication, March, 2005.
9. Ibid.
10. Ibid.
11. Wooden, *Practical modern basketball*, p. 25.
12. Gallimore & Tharp, What a coach can teach.
13. J. Wooden, personal communication, January, 2005.

14. No Child Left Behind Act of 2001. (2001, January). *Public Law No. 107–110, 107th Congress.* Retrieved April, 2005, from http://www.ed.gov/legislation/ESEA02/.
15. Ibid.
16. Goldenberg, *Successful school change*; Saunders & Goldenberg, The contribution of settings.

Chapter Six

1. J. Wooden, personal communication, April, 2005.
2. J. Wooden, personal communication, February 12, 2002.
3. J. Wooden, personal communication, May, 2004.
4. J. Wooden, personal communication, February 12, 2002.
5. Tharp & Gallimore, Basketball's John Wooden.
6. J. Wooden, personal communication, February 12, 2002.
7. Gallimore & Tharp, What a coach can teach.
8. Santagata, R. (2004) "Are you joking or are you sleeping?" Cultural beliefs and practices in Italian and U.S. teachers' mistake-handling strategies. *Linguistics and Education, 15*(1-2), 141-164.
9. Tharp & Gallimore, Basketball's John Wooden.
10. J. Wooden, personal communication, 2004.
11. J. Wooden, personal communication, 2003.
12. Ibid.
13. Bloom, B. S. (1986). The hands and feet of genius: Automaticity. *Educational Leadership*, February, 70-77.
14. Samuels, S. (2002). Reading fluency: Its development and assessment. In A. E. Farstrup & S. J. Samuels (Eds.), *What research has to say about reading instruction* (3rd ed., pp. 166–183). Newark, DE: International Reading Association, Inc.
15. National Council of Teachers of Mathematics (2005). *The learning principle.* Retrieved April, 2005, from http://standards.nctm.org/document/chapter2/learn.htm.

Chapter Seven

1. J. Wooden, personal communication, February 12, 2002.
2. Goldenberg, *Successful school change*; Black, P., & William, D. (1998). Assessment and classroom learning. *Assessment in Education: Principles, Policy and Practice, 5*(1), 7-74.
3. J. Wooden, personal communication, February 12, 2002.
4. Wooden, *Wooden: A lifetime of observations*, p. 199.
5. Tharp & Gallimore, Basketball's John Wooden.

6. J. Wooden, personal communication, 2003.
7. J. Wooden, personal communication, June, 2001.

Chapter Eight

1. Wooden, *My personal best*, p. 65.
2. J. Wooden, personal communication, February 12, 2002.
3. Ibid.
4. J. Wooden, personal communication, January, 2005.
5. Wooden, *Wooden: A lifetime of observations*, p. 197-201.
6. Damon, W. (1992). Teaching as moral craft and developmental expedition. In F. Oser, A. Dick, and J. L. Patry (Eds.), *Responsible and Effective Teaching*, (pp. 139-153). San Francisco: Jossey-Bass.
7. Hiebert, J., Gallimore, R., & Stigler, J. (2003). New heroes of the teaching profession. *Education Week, 23*(10), 56.
8. J. Wooden, personal communication, February 12, 2002.
9. J. Wooden, personal communication, July 11, 2003.
10. Johnson, *The John Wooden Pyramid of Success.*
11. Wooden, *My personal best.*
12. Bisheff, S. (2004). *John Wooden: An American treasure.* Nashville, TN: Cumberland House, p. 102.
13. Shackleton, J., & MacKenna, J. (2003). *Shackleton: An Irishman in Antarctica.* Madison: University of Wisconsin Press.
14. Wilcox, C. Quotation. Retrieved April, 2005, from http://www.zaadz.com/quotes/topics/teaching.
15. Johnson, *The John Wooden Pyramid of Success.*
16. Tharp & Gallimore, *Rousing minds to life.*
17. Gallimore & Tharp, What a coach can teach.
18. Tharp & Gallimore, Basketball's John Wooden, p. 78.

Index

D

demonstration, 91-92, 96-97
Dewey, John, 64
Dickinson, Roger, xviii
drills, 76, 99, 109
Duke University, 64
dunking, 81
Dwyre, Bill, xvii-xviii

E

"earned and deserved" approach, 15
 tardiness rule, 16
encouragement, 111-112
Erickson, Keith, xiii, 107
ESPN, xv
"exceptions to the rule." *See* outliers
experience, 121
explanation, 91-92, 96-97
extensions, 77

F

failing to prepare
 "a painful lesson," 67-72
 daily lesson plans and the organization of instruction, 75-82
   avoid altering a plan during a
    lesson, 81-82
   conditioning, 79-80
   end on a positive note, 80-81
   fundamentals before creativity, 75-76
   increasing complexity, 78-79
   quick transitions, 78
   teaching new material, 77-78
   use variety, 77
 plan for the week, 73-74
  preseason weekly plan, 73-74
  season weekly plan, 74
 plan for the year, 72-73
 planning and classroom teachers, 84-86

time management and organization,
  82-84
 patience, 83
 pattern, 83
 priority, 83
fairness, xxiii, 15, 17, 112
Fisher, Lee, 126
Frank G. Wells Disney award, xv
free-throw shooting (study of), 44-50
fundamentals, 50, 61, 90
 definition of, 75

G

Gallimore, Ronald, 93-95, 104, 111, 128,
 129
Gallimore, Sharon, xxiii
Givven, Karen, xxii
Glenn, John, 65
Goldenberg, Claude, xxii
Goodrich, Gail, xiii, 11, 13
"Grandfather of the Year" award, xv

H

Haberland, John, xxii
Hamlet (Shakespeare), 109, 115
Harmon, Glennice L., xvii
Hazzard, Walt, xiii, 11, 26
Henley, Mrs., 115
Hiebert, Jim, xxii
high-post offense, 56, 99, 114
Hill, Andy, 31-32
Hirsch, Jack, xiii

I

imaginary shooting, 4
imitation, 92-93, 96, 97
improvement through research
 data analysis, 48-49
 data collection, 47
 defining a research question, 44-45

T

teacher-student relationships
  "a life-long relationship is formed," 5-9
  learning about high expectations, 3-5
  relationships as the ends, not means, 17-20
  respect and fairness, 14-17
  "the relationship grows," 9-11
  "They are all different," 11-14
teaching
  and courage, 122-130
  as a moral profession, 121
  eleven common practices of good teaching, 108-114
    belief in students, 112-113
    deep subject knowledge, 110
    encouragement, 111-112
    engaging students, 109
    equal respect, 112
    fairness, 112
    individualized teaching, 114
    intensity, 111
    like being with students, 113-114
    organization, 110-111
    passion, 109-110
  favorite teachers, 106-107
  what special teachers have in common, 107-116
  "you haven't taught until they have learned," 103-106
team spirit, 35-37, 62-63
Tennessee, University of, 113
Tharp, Roland, xix, xxi, 93-95, 111, 128
The Athletic Journal, 44
The Declaration of Independence, 130
"The Great Competitor" (Rice), 38
"The New Math," 42
"The Wizard," xiii
"The Wizard of Westwood" (Chapin), 116

"They Ask Me Why I Teach" (Harmon), xvii
"This Is Your Life," x
time management, 82-84, 86-87
transitions, 78
Trgovich, Pete, 35-36

W

Walk of Hearts Teacher Recognition award, xv
Walton, Bill, xix, 3, 6-12, 31, 37, 51, 69, 72-73
"Walton Gang," 3, 72
Warren, Mike, 62
Warriner, Earl "Pop," xvi
Washington, Richard, 36
whole-part method, 90-91, 95
Wicks, Sydney, 16, 62-63, 73
Wilkes, Keith, 11, 72-73
Wooden, Joshua Hugh, xvi, 24
Wooden, Nell, xiii
"Woodens," 95

About the Authors

Photo courtesy of Belinda Thompson

Ronald Gallimore, John Wooden, and Swen Nater

Swen Nater, BS, is an assistant sporting goods buyer for Costco Wholesale. Along with his wife, Marlene Nater, he is a Phono-Graphix® reading therapist and trainer. They have a private practice in which they teach children to grasp the concepts and fluency of reading, spelling, and mathematics at all levels. From 1997-2003, he directed the Costco Wholesale corporate Employee Outreach Program, training Costco volunteers to help struggling readers in elementary schools across the United States and Canada catch up to their required grade level of reading. As a basketball player, Swen was a community college All-American in 1970 before playing behind NCAA Player of the Year Bill Walton under Coach John Wooden at UCLA, where he was a member of two UCLA national championship squads. He went on to become an NBA first-round draft pick in 1973 and the ABA Rookie of the Year in 1974. He led the ABA in rebounding in 1975, the NBA in 1980, and the Italian League in 1985. He still holds the NBA record for defensive rebounds in a half with 18. After his playing days, Swen taught algebra, sports psychology, and exercise psychology at Christian Heritage College while also serving as the school's athletic director and men's basketball coach from 1985-1995. In 1990, he and co-head coach Ray Slagle led Christian Heritage to its first NCCAA national championship. Swen and Wooden are co-authors of *John Wooden's UCLA Offense* (to be published in March 2006). He and James A. Peterson co-authored *The Complete Handbook of Rebounding—Fundamentals and Drills*. He has also produced three instructional basketball videos, *Rebounding: Simple and Effective, Unstoppable*, and *Not in My House*. Swen and Marlene, his wife of 32 years, reside in Enumclaw, Washington, and have two daughters: Alisha Yvonne (27) and Valerie Ann (26).

Ronald Gallimore, PhD, is Chief Scientist for LessonLab Research Institute and Distinguished Professor Emeritus at UCLA. He earned his BA from the University of Arizona and his PhD from Northwestern University. He taught psychology at California State University, Long Beach, and the University of Hawaii before joining the psychiatry faculty at UCLA in 1971. In 1966, he was appointed Research Psychologist at Princess Bernice Pauahi Bishop Museum to co-direct a five-year field study in a native Hawaiian community. In 1970, he and Roland Tharp designed a laboratory school (Kamehameha Elementary Education Project), which they co-directed for 10 years. For this work and their book *Rousing Minds to Life*, he and Tharp were presented the 1993 Grawemeyer Award in Education. In collaboration with Leslie Reese, Claude Goldenberg, and Estela Zarate, Ronald directed a 17-year study of immigrant Latino students and their families. He has collaborated with Goldenberg and Saunders on longitudinal studies of school and teaching improvement from 1985 to present. In 1992, he received a University of California Presidential Award for research contributing to the improvement of public schools. In 1993, the International Reading Association presented him and Goldenberg with the Albert J. Harris Award. In 1998, he and Jim Stigler founded LessonLab, which is devoted to the improvement of teaching through research and direct action in schools. Ronald co-directed the 1999 TIMSS Video Study and currently oversees research conducted at LessonLab (a Pearson Education Company: http://www.lessonlab.com). He has published five research monographs and more than 120 scholarly and scientific papers. Ronald and Sharon Gallimore were married in 1963, and have lived in Santa Monica since 1973. They have two daughters, Christine and Andrea, and two grandchildren, Julien and Cate.